Anonymous

An Historical Account of the Rise, Progress and present State of the Canal Navigation in Pennsylvania

With an Appendix Containing Abstracts of the Acts of the Legislature since the Year 1790...

Anonymous

An Historical Account of the Rise, Progress and present State of the Canal Navigation in Pennsylvania
With an Appendix Containing Abstracts of the Acts of the Legislature since the Year 1790...

ISBN/EAN: 9783744792011

Printed in Europe, USA, Canada, Australia, Japan

Cover: Foto ©ninafisch / pixelio.de

More available books at **www.hansebooks.com**

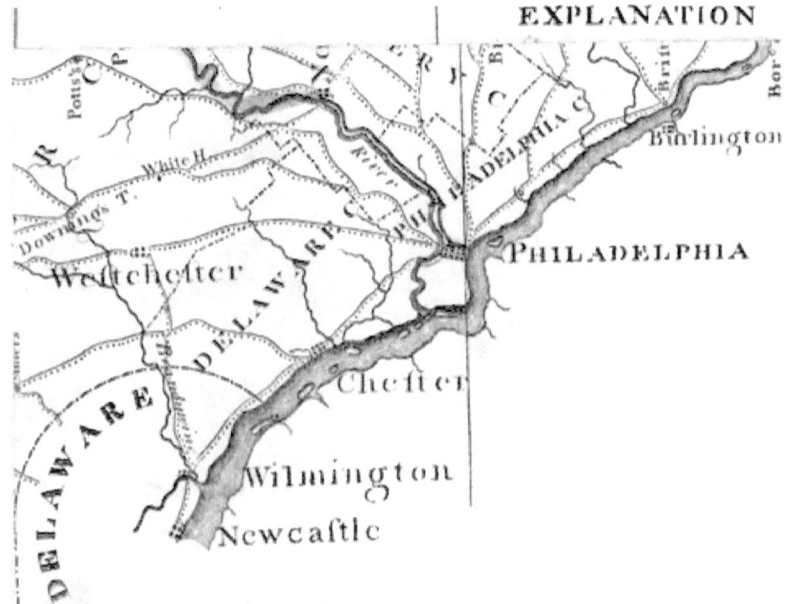

*…une, in the fifteenth Year of the Independence of the
…ffice the Title of a Map, the Right whereof he claims as
…nected therewith, relating to the Roads and inland
… from his larger Maps by Reading Howell. In Conform
…t of Learning by securing the Copies of Maps,
…ed. Sam.l Caldwell Clk. of the District of Pennsylvania*

AN
HISTORICAL ACCOUNT
OF THE
RISE, PROGRESS AND PRESENT STATE
OF
The Canal Navigation in Pennsylvania.
WITH AN APPENDIX,
CONTAINING,

Abstracts of the *Acts* of the *Legislature* since the Year 1790, and their Grants of Money for improving ROADS and NAVIGABLE WATERS throughout the State;

TO WHICH IS ANNEXED,

"AN EXPLANATORY MAP."

PUBLISHED BY DIRECTION OF THE PRESIDENT AND MANAGERS OF THE SCHUYLKILL AND SUSQUEHANNA, AND THE DELAWARE AND SCHUYLKILL NAVIGATION COMPANIES.

" Here smooth CANALS, across th' extended plain
Stretch their long arms to join the distant *main*.
The Sons of Toil, with many a weary stroke,
Scoop the hard bosom of the solid rock;
Resistless through the stiff, opposing c'ay.
With steady patience, work their gradual way;
Compel the Genius of th' unwilling flood,
Through the brown horrors of the aged wood,
Cross the lone waste the silver urn they pour,
And cheer the barren heath, or sullen moor.
The traveller, with pleasing wonder, sees
The white sail gleaming through the dusky trees;

And views the alter'd landscape with surprize,
And doubts the magic scenes which round him rise.
Now, like a flock of swans, above his head,
Their woven wings the flying vessels spread;
Now, meeting streams, in artful mazes, glide,
While each, unmingled, pours a separate tide;
Now, through the hidden veins of earth they flow,
And visit sulphurous mines and caves below.
The ductile streams obey the guiding hand,
And *social Plenty* crowns the HAPPY LAND!"

PHILADELPHIA:

PRINTED BY ZACHARIAH POULSON, JUNIOR, NUMBER EIGHTY, CHESNUT-STREET.

M DCC XCV.

AN HISTORICAL ACCOUNT

OF THE

RISE, PROGRESS AND PRESENT STATE

OF

The Canal Navigation in Pennsylvania.

WITH AN APPENDIX,

CONTAINING,

Abstracts of the *Acts* of the *Legislature* since the Year 1790, and their Grants of Money for improving ROADS and NAVIGABLE WATERS throughout the State;

TO WHICH IS ANNEXED,

"AN EXPLANATORY MAP."

PUBLISHED BY DIRECTION OF THE PRESIDENT AND MANAGERS OF THE SCHUYLKILL AND SUSQUEHANNA, AND THE DELAWARE AND SCHUYLKILL NAVIGATION COMPANIES.

" Here smooth CANALS, across th' extended plain
Stretch their long arms to join the distant *main*.
The Sons of Toil, with many a weary stroke,
Scoop the hard bosom of the solid rock;
Resistless through the stiff, opposing c'ay.
With steady patience, work their gradual way;
Compel the Genius of th' unwilling flood,
Through the brown horrors of the aged wood;
Cross the lone waste the silver urn they pour,
And cheer the barren heath, or sullen moor.
The traveller, with pleasing wonder, sees
The white sail gleaming through the dusky trees;

And views the alter'd landscape with surprize,
And doubts the magic scenes which round him rise.
Now, like a flock of swans, above his head,
Their woven wings the flying vessels spread;
Now, meeting streams, in artful mazes, glide,
While each, unmingled, pours a separate tide;
Now, through the hidden veins of earth they flow,
And visit sulphurous mines and caves below
The ductile streams obey the guiding hand,
And *social Plenty* crowns the HAPPY LAND!"

PHILADELPHIA:

PRINTED BY ZACHARIAH POULSON, JUNIOR, NUMBER EIGHTY, CHESNUT-STREET.

M DCC XCV.

Officers of the Schuylkill and Susquehanna Navigation Company.	Officers of the Delaware and Schuylkill Canal Company.
President.	**President.**
Robert Morris.	Robert Morris.
Managers.	**Managers.**
David Rittenhouse,	David Rittenhouse,
John Nicholson,	John Nicholson,
William Smith, D. D.	William Smith, D. D.
William Bingham,	William Bingham,
Standish Forde,	Standish Forde,
John Steinmetz,	Joseph Ball,
Samuel Meredith,	Jeremiah Parker,
Walter Stewart,	Robert Hare,
Joseph Ball,	Benjamin R. Morgan,
Thomas Ruston,	Walter Stewart,
Jeremiah Parker,	Charles G. Paleski,
Francis West.	Samuel Meredith.
Treasurer.	**Treasurer.**
Tench Francis.	Tench Francis.
Secretary.	**Secretary.**
Timothy Matlack.	William Moore Smith.

ADDENDUM.

N. B. In the *Map*, the artificial *Canal* work is colored with *Red*, and where the natural and improved beds of the rivers are to be used, they are colored *Blue*.

The READER is requested to make the following CORRECTIONS:—

In page xi of the *Introduction*, last line, for "rivers" read "rivals." In page xii, line 16, before the word "junction," insert "the." In page xiii, line 23, for "Stretford" read "Setford." In page xv, the last line except one, for "measures" read "minerals."

In page 22 of the work itself, line 17, for "yet *they would make*," &c. read "but *they*," &c. and line 22, for "*but*" read "*and*." Page 62, column 2, line 9, after the words "20 men," and before the word "horses," for "18" read "80." Page 64, line 14, after the word "years" read as follows, *viz.* "The sum already expended amounts to £. 52,500." Page 65, last line, for "bank" read "banks." Page 68, line 9, for "*John*" read "*Thomas*." Page 72, in the 5th. line from the bottom, for "*and* a grievous" insert "*but* a grievous."

INTRODUCTION.

COMMERCE, between the inhabitants of different countries, as regulated by the *general laws* of NATURE and NATIONS, and by *particular treaties*, is the furest means of uniting all mankind, in one happy bond of civilization, peace and prosperity.

By COMMERCE, in this enlarged sense of the word, "the whole world becomes, as it were, one single family." What Nature has denied to the inhabitants of one climate, is supplied by what she has liberally bestowed on another; and the super-abundance of each becomes *common stock*.

What COMMERCE, considered in this view, is to mankind in general, by means of *foreign trade* and *external navigation*; she is, in a smaller degree, to particular states and societies, by means of *inland navigation* and *good roads*; whereby the produce of one part of the country, as the case may require, is easily exchanged for that of another, and the superfluities of the whole readily carried to the principal marts or seaports for exportation.

Without improvements of this kind, together with a good government and laws for the encouragement of *industry* and *protection* of property, the inhabitants of countries rich by nature, capable of being bound together in one flourishing and civilized *whole*, sensible of a common interest, and rejoicing in the common prosperity, may continue long in a state of almost savage wretchedness and poverty, insensible to the benefits of social and civil life, contributing *scantily* to the relief of their own wants, and *nothing* to relieve the wants of others, or to increase the common stock of felicity in their own country, and of the world in general.

When a country is well improved by means of *good roads* and *canals*, joining its principal rivers, and thus establishing a general *inland communication*; each district with its superfluity may, as already mentioned, purchase what it wants of another, and each be reciprocally furnished with all necessaries and commodities; and, therefore, improvements of this kind are among the strongest marks of the good policy of a nation.

Canals

Canals and *water-carriage*, in particular (as is well observed by the writers on this subject) "render land-carriages and beasts of burthen less necessary; and they may be more profitably employed in tillage and agriculture. By *canals*, dry and barren grounds are fertilized, and marshy and watery grounds are drained. By means of them, manufactures require fewer hands and less expense; and traffic is extended and animates all parts of a country, procuring plenty and happiness to the individuals, and enlarging the power and strength of a state or sovereignty in general."

"In fine, by *canals*, a people may be supplied," in their cities, towns, and elsewhere, "with grain, forage, fuel, materials for building, and also all other heavy and raw materials for manufactures, which otherwise would remain of little value at a distance from the place where they are wanted, because of the great expense commonly attending their transportation by carriages, &c. for, a *barge* of a reasonable size, worked by two men and drawn by two horses, can transport seventy or eighty tons; which weight, by any other carriage, would have required forty men and about one hundred and sixty horses." This calculation is made for the canals in England, where, by means of turnpikes, a level country and improved roads, land-carriage has a great advantage over any land-carriage that can, for many years, be compleated throughout the greatest part of the United States; and the calculations are also verified by considering the difference between land and water-carriage in the immense commerce carried on by *canals* in Holland, France and Italy. To estimate the difference of expense between *land* and *water-carriage* in *Pennsylvania*, while our rivers continue in an unimproved state, is difficult. An estimate, however, was attempted for this purpose, founded on the most authentic documents, and laid before the Legislature in February, 1791,* as may be seen from page 11th. to page 17th. of the following papers, and was greatly in favor of water-carriage. But when the canals, now in operation, shall be compleated, even to the connection of the city of Philadelphia with Presqu' Isle on lake Erie (two short portages only excepted) the difference in favor of water-carriage, it is probable, will be far greater than is estimated in England, Holland, France and Italy, or indeed any other European country.

It

---

* The plan of a more accurate estimate will be added to the report of the engineer, for the year 1794, in the subsequent papers.

(v)

It is no wonder then, that from the earliest stages of *commerce* in the Old World, and even for the conveniency of military expeditions, and maneuvres both of attack and defence, *canals* for water-carriage should have been among the first improvements made on the face of nature, by the most powerful states, both ancient and modern.

Among the *canals* executed by the ANCIENTS, the first mentioned by historians is that which connected the *Red Sea* and the *Mediterranean;* by which, it is said, *king Solomon* passed with his fleet to join that of *Hyram*, king of Tyre, to proceed together to *Ophir* in search of gold, as in Kings, I. chap. 9th. *Herodotus*, *Diodorus* and *Strabo* among the ancients; *Delisle*, Father *Sicard* and *Rollin* among the moderns, have all borne testimony to the existence of this canal; and its ruins have been traced by sundry travellers—*Rollin*, in particular, gives the following account of it—

" The *canal* which joined the *Red Sea* and *Mediterranean*, is not one of the least advantages which the *Nile* afforded *Egypt*. This *canal* had its beginning near the town of *Bubastus*; it was one hundred cubits, that is, fifty yards broad, so that two boats could pass with ease, deep enough for the largest vessels, and above one hundred *stadia*, that is, fifty leagues long." But this canal, useful and extensive as it is said to have been, can hardly be compared, in point of utility or extent, to what may be anticipated in the future prospects of *commerce* in the UNITED STATES, by means of *canals* and *rivers* joining the tide-waters of Delaware, Susquehanna, Potomack, Hudson's river, &c. with the Ohio, Mississippi, the great western lakes, and perhaps the South sea itself.

It would be foreign to the main subject of the following papers, to speak of the military *canals* of the *Romans;* such as the *Fossa Mariana* to draw subsistence by sea up the *Rhone;* the canal from the *Isser* (which empties into the *Zuyder-zee*) to the *Rhone* and *Rhine;* the canal joining the river *Nyne* in England, near *Peterborough*, with the *Witham* below *Lincoln*. But it may be proper to observe, that even in a *military* as well as *commercial* view, it may be worthy of the *United States* of America, to improve the natural advantages of their situation along our *sea coasts*, as well as in the *internal* parts of our country. For example, if it should ever be the misfortune of these states to be engaged in a foreign war

b

war, especially with maritime powers, how easy and safe might a water communication be made from Rhode Island and the eastern states to New York; and from New York to Philadelphia, by joining the *Millstone* or other branches of the *Rariton* with the river Delaware and the city of Philadelphia; and then from Philadelphia down the Delaware, and (by a short cut of about four miles and a half below Newcastle) from the Delaware to Chesapeak bay, *Baltimore*, *Annapolis* and the city of *Washington* on Potomack; thence still by bays, canals and cuts, through Virginia, North and South Carolina to Savannah in Georgia. In time of *war*, this might not only give a safe communication from one extremity of the United States to another, similar to the communication from province to province and from town to town in Holland, free from the interruption of the privateers of a foreign enemy; but even in time of *peace* such a communication, at certain seasons, by vessels not fit for a *coasting* trade, and the danger of doubling capes and going out to *sea*, might answer many commercial purposes, and make shorter and safer voyages—But this hint is only thrown out hastily, and by the bye. We return to the subject of *ancient* and *modern* canals for *internal* navigation.

Next to the *canals* of the ancients, already mentioned, and indeed superior in name to any of them, is the CANAL OF CHINA, begun about the end of the third century; which is said to be the source of immense riches, being constantly covered with a multitude of vessels and boats; by which one may travel, within land, from *Pekin* to the extremity of the empire—a space of six hundred leagues. " The principal canal discharges itself on both sides, into a great number of others, which accommodate the most part of the towns and villages, and answer the conveniency of travellers and traffick. The small *canals* are again subdivided into a number of smaller to fertilize the neighboring plains. Travellers speak with extacy of this *canal*, and of the magnificence and beauty of the *stone bridges* over the same, the piers being so slender, by the goodness of the materials, that the arches, which are very high, appear at a distance, as if suspended in the air; and, when many can be seen at once, they form a prospect the most agreeable in the world: yet these ingenious people have not the use of locks and sluices, but by the help of ropes and pullies, draw their boats up dams of masonry, where there is a fall, which is sometimes attended with great danger."

Of MODERN CANALS, those of *France* deserve particular notice. "As early as the reign of their Henry IV. the French became sensible of the great advantages the Dutch and Flemings enjoyed by joining rivers and seas by *canals;* and therefore conceived many projects of this kind. The most important of those executed are the following—

I. The *canal* for joining the *Seine* and *Loire,* which was the first made in that country, with locks and sluices to ascend and descend boats, without the labor and danger of ropes and pullies, as in the ancient method.

II. The *canal* of *Orleans,* to aid the former, as of great importance to the city of Paris; and which meets the Loire a little above Orleans and was finished in 1724, making the navigation of the *Seine,* from near *Orleans,* as good as can be desired.

III. But of all the great works executed in France, the CANAL OF LANGUEDOC, called also the *canal* of the two seas, is the greatest, and reflects more honor on *Lewis* the XIV. than all the victories and spendid acts of his reign. By means of this grand *canal,* a ready communication is made between the two fertile provinces of *Guyenne* and *Languedoc,* and in consequence between the *Atlantic* and *Mediterranean.* " It is sixty-four leagues long, and has one hundred and four locks, extending in some places for a mile together by a passage dug through rocks under ground. The expense was thirteen millions of livres, of which the king contributed seven millions, and the province of Languedoc the rest [*See Savare Dict. Comm.*] " And if the king, on the representation of *Colebert,* had not shared the expense, and magnificently given the perpetual revenues of it to the celebrated engineer, Mr. *Riquet* and his heirs, subject only to the sole charge of keeping it in repair, this great work had, perhaps, remained unfinished to this day. The states of *Languedoc,* with equal magnanimity, contributed their part, by a tax on that province, without any view to a share of the profits; excepting so far that they rightly considered, the tax as continuing only for a time, but that the expenditures of the profits, would be amongst themselves, and continue a permanent source of riches, increasing more and more, by the advantages they would reap from trade, added to that of obtaining with ease, those things which they stood in most need of—and the event confirmed their expectations."

" The

" The *opposition* which Mr. *Riquet* met with from the OWNERS OF THE GROUND, through which the *canal* was to pass, being made known to *Colebert*, he thought the only way to avoid these difficulties, was to engage the king to *indemnify all those who might think themselves aggrieved;* who, accordingly, took the canal into his own protection, bought the ground through which it was to pass, erected it into a fief, and gave the property to Mr. Riquet, as aforesaid."

A similar opposition has been made by some of the owners of lands on the route of the Pennsylvania canals; but this, it is hoped, may be overcome gradually by the good sense of the people: if not, the remedy is in the power of the Legislature by an amendment of the incorporating acts, providing more effectually for a valuation by *good and lawful men indifferent to the parties.*

But to return to some further account of the *Languedoc canal*, which, traversing an immense tract of country, and joining two oceans by an entire inland navigation, bears the greatest similitude (although upon a shorter scale) to the *canals* proposed for joining the *Atlantic ocean* by means of the tide waters of *Hudson*'s river, the *Delaware*, *Susquehanna* and *Potomack* on the east, with *Ohio* or *Mississippi*, and the great lakes, which are in the nature of *oceans*, on the *west*.

The *Languedoc canal* (according to the account of VALLENCEY, an able engineer, whose authority is made use of in many parts of this introduction) is " divided into two principal parts, running from its * *point of partage*, which is the most elevated spot in the neighborhood of *Castlenaudari*. The *first*, which extends ninety-six thousand three hundred and

---

* The *point of portage*, is that point on the summit of some mountain, or highest middle ground where the waters, head springs, or sources of different great rivers rise; and, dividing themselves, run different ways. Thus, in the navigation from Philadelphia, by means of the *Schuylkill*, *Susquehanna* and *Juniata* rivers on the *east* side, and the *Conemaugh*, *Kiskeminetas*, *Allegheny* and its branch called *French creek*, on the *west* side, [See the map] by which the tide waters of *Delaware* may be connected with *Lake Erie* (and the other great lakes) at *Presqu' Isle*; and with the *Mississippi* waters, at the heads of Conemaugh; the point of partage is on a fine level on the Allegheny mountain, where large springs running *eastward* into the *Juniata branch* of *Susquehanna*, and *westward* into the *Conemaugh* branch of *Allegheny* river, and consequently of the *Ohio*, and *Mississippi*, are but a few rods apart; and the present carrying place from the mouth of Poplar run on Juniata to the forks of Little Conemaugh, less than sixteen miles.

and fifteen French fathoms towards the *Mediterranean*, descends from the point of partage to the lake of *Thau* near *Agde*, and passes from thence to the port of *Cette* in the *Mediterranean*. The *second*, which extends twenty-nine thousand three hundred and sixty-six fathoms, descends from the *point of partage* to the ocean at its mouth in the *Garonne*, below *Toulouse*; so that between the two mouths of this grand canal, the whole extent is one hundred and twenty-five thousand six hundred and eighty-one fathoms, or fifty French leagues and an half. An exact level of the ground being taken, it was found that the point of partage was six hundred French feet higher than the lake of *Thau*, which is on a level with the Mediterranean, and one hundred and eighty-six French feet above the mean height of the *Garonne*, taken immediately below Toulouse."

" To pass the boats from the port of *Cette* up to the *point of partage*, there are seventy-four locks,† of about eight feet fall each; and twenty-six locks from the same point to the *Garonne*, which is navigable from Toulouse to the ocean; so that this CANAL contains one hundred *great locks*. The only difficulty in the accomplishment of this work (for the ground is level and of a good kind) was the expense, which was supplied as above stated.

" Of these one hundred locks, the most beautiful are the *eight locks* together, near *Beziers*, which form one continued cascade of one hundred and fifty fathoms long and sixty-six French feet fall; that is eight feet three inches fall to each lock."—Similar to this, and equally beautiful, are the *five locks* together, at the east end of the summit level of the *Schuylkill* and *Susquehanna canal*, between *Myers-town*, near the head of the Tulpehocken branch of *Schuylkill;* and *Lebanon*, at the head of the *Quittapahilla* and *Swatara* branch of *Susquehanna*. Here there is thirty feet fall, that is six feet fall to each lock, comprized in the

distance

---

† To pass from the *summit level* of the *Schuylkill* and *Susquehanna canal* to the mouth of *Tulpehocken* on Schuylkill eastward, in the distance of near thirty-five miles, the fall is three hundred and ten feet, proposed to be divided into forty-five locks—The descent from the *west* end of the summit level to the *Susquehanna*, at the mouth of its *Swatara* branch, has not yet been finally ascertained, nor, consequently, the number of locks, should it be eventually necessary to make a *canal* and locks the whole way, and every where to quit the bed of the river.

distance of three hundred and seventy feet; by which junction there is a saving of about a fifth of the expense which would have been requisite in the construction of so many locks separately.

"In the *route* of the *Languedoc canal*, there are several hills and mountains in the aforesaid space of fifty leagues, which the *canal* was to cross; all of which are cut through, except that of *Malpas*; which, being very high and rocky, is hollowed, or tunnelled, in the form of a vault, with a foot bank four feet broad, to draw the boats along. This work passes for as extraordinary and noble a thing as any of the ancient Romans."

"This *canal* (of *Languedoc*) is sixty feet broad at top, thirty feet at bottom, and six feet deep. At the *point* of *partage*, there is the great *bason* called *Narouse* of an octangular form, being four hundred yards long, three hundred broad and seven feet deep, its sides lined with masonry—The greatest difficulty in joining the two seas by means of this canal, was thought to be that of finding a sufficient quantity of water at the *point* of *partage*, to supply a continual navigation of fifty leagues, because of the inevitable loss by the gates, the oozing and evaporation. It was here that *Riquet* gave proof of his superior abilities, for providing for so essential an article, by the * reservoir of *St. Farriol*, the greatest work that has been executed by the moderns—This he accomplished by means of a trench collecting the waters which rise and descend from the *black mountain*, into the grand reservoir at the summit level, or point of partage. The waters of this reservoir, run out through large brass cocks, which communicate with vaulted galleries, made at the bottom of the dam, one hundred feet below the surface."

"In constructing this grand canal, they inevitably crossed many rivers and rivulets; and then thought of no other expedient than to bring them into

---

* This reservoir is said to contain a body of water, whose superficies is two millions three hundred and forty thousand square feet and one hundred feet depth, which makes above one million cubic fathoms of water. The reservoir and locks on the summit level of the *Schuylkill* and *Susquehanna canal* are supplied by the head springs of *Tulpehocken*, which empties into the *Schuylkill* branch of DELAWARE, and the head springs of the Quittapahilla and Swatara branch of SUSQUEHANNA. An estimate of the quantity of water, which these head springs will carry into the reservoir at the *summit level*, will be found in the following papers.

into it, and let them overflow again at particular places, that they might always keep a sufficient depth of water for the navigation; and so far from thinking these foreign waters an inconvenience, they were considered as proper to supply what was lost by evaporation. At the end of some years they found their error; for the mud, which these foreign waters brought into the canal, increased so fast, that the canal would not have remained long navigable, had not the celebrated engineer *Vauban*, found means to separate these foreign waters from the *canal*, and to let in as much of them as they pleased, and when they thought proper. This he compleated by *back drains*, or side ditches, and aqueducts of his own invention—There are forty-five of these on this canal, which are of two kinds; the first, called aqueduct bridges, raised on arches, to support the canal, under which passes these foreign rivers and waters. There are thirty-nine others, passing syphon-wise* from one side ditch to another under the canal. There are many other *canals*, which it would be needless to describe on this occasion; such as that of *Grave* navigable to *Montpellier* and from thence by the river *Lez* to the sea; that of *Lunel*, emptying itself likewise into the sea; those of *Radelle*, *Burgogne* and *Silvestal*, communicating from *Aiguemorte* on the Rhine to the sea; the canal of *Novella*, crossing the lakes of *Salces*, *Palme* and *Signeau* from the neighborhood of *Perpignan* to *Narbonne*, from thence to the river *Aude*, within one league of the great *canal*; the whole facilitating one great and various communication, from the mouth of the *Rhone* to *Perpignan*, and to the ocean, without running any risks by sea.

It would be likewise needless to describe, or even to attempt, on this occasion, to enumerate all the canals, made in *Holland* and the *Netherlands*, within the two last centuries, for the benefit of commerce. The whole country exhibits one chain of water carriage, for profit as well as pleasure, from port to port, and from town to town, and from village to village, through these countries. " Even under the government of a *woman*, *Elizabeth Eugenia*, in the low countries, one hundred and seventy years ago the famous *canal of St. Mery* was made; which joins the *Rhine* and the *Meuse*, extending from *Rheinberg* to *Vanlo*, in order to transport all the merchandize, which comes from *Germany* into Brabant, and to deprive the Dutch of that trade; foreseeing the jealousy that this work would create amongst her Dutch rivers in trade, she caused

it

---

* Commonly called *Culverts*.

it to be fortified by twenty-four redoubts of defence, to support the workmen in case they should be molested; and although the prince of Orange attacked them several times, he could not prevent the work from being perfected."

" In addition to this, it may not be improper to mention the exertions of the Czar, PETER I. who of all the sovereigns who have endeavored to polish and enrich an almost barbarous multitude of subjects, justly merited the title of *great*. This prince travelled through *England, Holland, Germany* and *France*, to instruct himself in military discipline, trade, navigation and the art of government; and having engaged many learned and skilful persons of foreign nations, in his service, contemplated, in imitation of France, by internal navigation, to join the seas which surround his kingdom."

" The principal rivers of *Russia* are the *Dwina*, which falls into the *White Sea*, the *Don* into the *Baltic*, and the *Wolga* into the *Caspian Sea*. The Czar thought that junction of these rivers by *canals*, would give his subjects a communication with all the seas; and after going himself over this vast tract, having taken all the levels, resolved on the places of the canals for their junction—in a word, having planned every thing for so great a project, he began by the junction of the *Wolga* with *Wolkava*, which empties into the lake *Ladoga*, running by *Petersburg* into the *Baltic Sea*. In this manner, it was practicable *to cross all Russia by water*, which is above eight hundred leagues from the *Baltic* to the *Caspian Sea*. The intention of this *monarch* was that *Petersburg*, by its favorable situation, should become a magazine for the commerce of the whole world, which would probably have happened, if he had not died in one thousand seven hundred and twenty-five, before the completion of his projects."

In *England, Scotland* and *Ireland*, it may be unnecessary to observe what facilities have been given to *trade* and *commerce*, by means of *roads* and *canals*—mountains have been traversed and levelled for *land-carriage*, and, where necessary, *perforated* for *water-carriage;* rivers running contrary courses, and seas washing opposite shores, have been made to embrace each other, and an easy and cheap *inland navigation* formed through all parts of the insular dominion. The joining the *friths* of *Forth* and
Clyde

Clyde in *Scotland*, and the *duke* of *Bridgewater's navigation*, not to mention a multitude of others, in England, might be adduced as examples. Of the latter, namely—the duke of Bridgewater's, the re-publication of a short extract from memoirs of the life of Mr. *James Brindley*, may be proper to show that neither mountains nor valleys, rivers nor marshes, can be any long impediment to skill and perseverance, supplied and supported by adequate finances.

" The duke of Bridgewater hath at Worsley, about seven miles from Manchester, a large estate, rich with mines of coal, which had hitherto lain useless in the bowels of the earth, because the expense of carriage was too great to find a market for consumption.

" The duke, wishing to work these mines, perceived the necessity of a canal from Worsley to Manchester: upon which occasion, Mr. Brindley, who was now become famous in the country, was consulted. Having surveyed the ground, he declared the scheme to be practicable. In consequence of this, an act was obtained in the years 1758 and 1759, for enabling the duke to cut a canal from Worsley to Salford, near Manchester, and to carry the same to or near Hollin Ferry, in the county of Lancaster. It being, however, afterwards discovered, that the navigation would be more beneficial, both to the duke of Bridgewater and the public, if carried over the river Irwell, near Barton bridge, to Manchester—he applied again to parliament, and procured an act, which enabled him to vary the course of the canal agreeably to this new plan, and likewise to extend a side branch to Longford bridge in Stretford. Mr. Brindley in the mean time had begun these great undertakings, being the first of the kind ever attempted in England, with navigable subterraneous tunnels and elevated aqueducts. The principle laid down at the commencement of this business reflects much honor on the noble undertaker, as well as upon his engineer. It was resolved that the canal should be perfect in its kind, and that, in order to preserve the level of the water, it should be free from the usual obstructions of locks. But, in accomplishing this end, many difficulties occurred, which were deemed unsurmountable. It was necessary that the canal should be carried over rivers, and many large and deep vallies, where it was evident that such stupendous mounds of earth must be raised as could scarcely, it was thought, be completed by the labor of ages; and above all, it was not known from what source so large a supply of water could be drawn, as, even upon this improved plan, would be requisite for the navigation. But Mr. Brindley, with a strength of mind peculiar to himself, and being possessed of the confidence of his great patron, conquered all the embarrassments thrown in his way, not only from the nature of the undertaking itself, but by the passions and prejudices of interested individuals, and the admirable machines he contrived, and the methods he took, to facilitate the progress of the work, brought on such a rapid execution of it, that the world began to wonder how it could have been esteemed so difficult.

" When

"When the canal was compleated as far as Barton, where the Irwell is navigable for large vessels, Mr. Brindley proposed to carry it over that river, by an aqueduct of thirty-nine feet above the surface of the water. This, however, being generally considered as a wild and extravagant project, he desired, in order to justify his conduct towards his noble employer, that the opinion of another engineer might be taken; believing that he could easily convince an intelligent person of the practicability of his design. A gentleman of eminence was accordingly called in; who, being conducted to the place where it was intended that the aqueduct should be made, ridiculed the attempt; and when the height and dimensions were communicated to him, he exclaimed, I have often heard of castles in the air, but never before was shown where any of them were to be erected.

"This unfavorable verdict did not deter the duke of Bridgewater from following the opinion of his own engineer. The aqueduct was immediately begun; and it was carried on with such rapidity and success, as astonished all those who had but a little before condemned it as a chimerical scheme.

"This work commenced in September, 1760; and the first boat sailed over on the 17th. July, 1761. From that time, it was not uncommon to see a boat loaded with forty tons drawn over the aqueduct, with great ease, by one or two mules; while below, against the stream of the Irwell, persons had the pain of beholding ten or twelve men tugging at an equal draught; a striking instance of the superiority of a canal navigation over that of a river not in the tide way. The works were then extended to Manchester, at which place the curious machines for landing coals upon the top of the hill, gives a pleasing idea of Mr. Brindley's address in diminishing labour by mechanical contrivances.

"The duke of Bridgewater perceiving, more and more, the importance of these inland navigations, not only to himself in particular, but to the community in general, extended his ideas to Liverpool; and though he had every difficulty to encounter, that could arise from the novelty of his undertakings, his grace happily overcame all opposition, and obtained, in 1762, an act of parliament for branching his canal to the tide way of the Mersy—This part of the canal is carried over the Mersy and Bollen, and over many wide and deep vallies Over the vallies it is conducted without the assistance of a single lock; the level of the water being preserved by raising a mound of earth, and forming therein a channel for the water across the valley at Setford, through which the Mersy runs: this kind of work extends nearly a mile.

"A person might naturally have been led to conclude, that the conveyance of such a mass of earth must have employed all the horses and carriages in the country, and that the completion of it would be the business of an age. But our excellent mechanic made his canal subservient to this part of his design, and brought the soil in boats of a peculiar construction, which was conducted into caissoons or cisterns. On opening the bottom of the boats, the earth was deposited where it was wanted; and thus, in the easiest and simplest manner, the valley was elevated to a proper level for continuing the canal. The ground across the Bollen was raised by temporary locks, which were formed of the timber used in the caissoons, just mentioned. In the execution of
every

every part of the navigation, Mr. Brindley produced many valuable machines, which ought never to be forgot in this kingdom; nor ought the œconomy, and forecast, which are apparent through the whole work, to be omitted, in the stops, or floodgates, fixed in the canal where it is above the level of the land. The stops are so constructed, that, should any of the banks give way, and thereby occasion a current, the adjoining gates will rise by that motion only, and prevent any other part of the water from escaping, except that which is near the breach between the two gates— The success with which the duke of Bridgewater's undertakings were crowned, encouraged a number of gentlemen, and manufacturers, in Staffordshire, to revive the idea of a canal navigation through that country, for the conveying to market at a cheaper rate, the products and manufactures of the interior parts of the kingdom. This plan was patronized by lord Gower and Mr. Anson; and met with the concurrence of many persons of rank, fortune, and influence in the neighbouring counties. Mr. Brindley was, therefore, engaged to make a survey from the Trent to the Mersy; and upon his reporting that is was practicable to construct a canal, from one of those rivers to the other, and thereby to unite the ports of Liverpool and Hull, a subscription for carrying it into execution was set on foot in 1765, and an act of parliament* was obtained in the same year.

" In 1766, this canal, called by the proprietors, " the canal from the Trent to the Mersy," but more emphatically by the engineer, " the grand trunk navigation," on account of the numerous branches which he justly supposed would be extended every way from it, was begun; and under his direction conducted with great spirit and success, as long as he lived. Mr. Brindley's life not being continued to the completion of this important and arduous undertaking, he left it to be finished by his brother-in-law, Mr. Henshall, who put the last hand to it in May, 1777, being somewhat less that eleven years after its commencement. We need not say, that the final execution of the grand trunk navigation gave the highest satisfaction to the proprietors, and excited a general joy in a populous country, the inhabitants of which already receive every advantage they could wish from so truly noble an enterprise.

" This canal is 93 miles in length, and, besides a large number of bridges over it, has 76 locks and 5 tunnels. The most remarkable of the tunnels is a subterraneous passage of Harecastle, being 2880 yards in length, and more than 70 yards below the surface of the earth. The scheme of this inland navigation had employed the thoughts of the ingenious part of the kingdom for upwards of twenty years before, and some surveys had been made; but Harecastle hill, through which the tunnel is conducted, could neither be avoided nor overcome by any expedient the ablest engineers could devise. It was Mr. Brindley alone who surmounted such difficulties, arising from the variety of measures, strata and quicksands, as no one but himself would have attempted to conquer.

" Soon

---

* He was the greatest enthusiast in favor of artificial navigations that ever existed. Having spoken upon various circumstances of rivers before a committee of the House of Commons, in which he seemed to treat all sorts of rivers with great contempt, a member asked him, for what purpose he apprehended rivers were created? Brindley, considering with himself a little before he gave an answer, replied at last, " to feed navigable canals."

" Soon after the navigation from the Trent to the Mersey was undertaken, application was made to parliament, by the gentlemen of Staffordshire and Worcestershire, for leave to construct a canal from the grand trunk, near Haywood, in Staffordshire, to the river Severn, near Bewly. The act being obtained, the design was executed by our great engineer; and hereby the port of Bristol was added to the two before united ports of Liverpool and Hull. This canal, which is about 46 miles in length, was compleated in 1772. Mr. Brindley's next undertaking was the survey and execution of a canal from Birmingham, to unite with Staffordshire and Worcestershire canal, near Wolverhampton. This navigation, which was finished in about three years, is 26 miles in length. As by means of it vast quantities of coal are conveyed to the river Severn, as well as to Birmingham, where there must be a peculiar demand for them, extraordinary advantages have accrued to manufactures and commerce.

" Our engineer advised the proprietors of the last mentioned navigation, in order to avoid the inconvenience of locks, and to supply the canal more effectually with water, to have a tunnel at Smethwick. This would have rendered it a compleat work. But his advice was rejected; and to supply the deficiency, the managers have lately erected two of Messrs. Watts and Boulton's steam engines. The canal from Droitwich to the river Severn, for the conveyance of salt and coal, was likewise executed by Mr. Brindley. By him also the Coventry navigation was planned, and it was a short time under his direction.

" The Canal from Chesterfield to the river Trent, at Stockwith, was the last public undertaking in which Mr. Brindley engaged.

" And notwithstanding *some of the canals passed through the fine villas and extensive lawns of many gentlemen's retreats*, yet *their* MAGNANIMITY induced them to sacrifice their private convenience for public utility.*

" He surveyed and planned the whole, and executed some miles of the navigation, which was successfully finished by Mr. Henshall in 1777.

" The last of our great mechanic's ingenuity and uncommon contrivances that we shall mention, is his improvement of the machine for drawing water out of mines, by a loosing and gaining bucket. This he afterwards employed to advantage in raising up coal from the mines."

* Persons were offered to be appointed to value the ground, and assess damages, which they refused.

P. S. Upon an extensive view of the natural advantages, which Pennsylvania enjoys, for improvements of this kind, a few of her citizens, in the year 1789, united by the name of " The SOCIETY for promoting the improvement of ROADS and INLAND NAVIGATION;" and the number of members soon increased to more than *one hundred*, residing in various parts of the state; whose meetings were to be on every Monday evening, during the session of the Legislature, in order to suggest information, schemes and proposals, for promoting internal trade, manufactures and population, by facilitating every possible communication between the different parts of the state.

The following are the principal memorials, which have hitherto been acted upon by the *Legislature*, so far as concerns land and water-carriage.

To the honorable the Senate and House of Representatives of the Freemen of the commonwealth of Pennsylvania, in General Assembly met.

The memorial of " The Society for promoting the improvement of roads and inland navigation,"

Respectfully sheweth,

THAT your memorialists, residing in various parts of this state, with a view to contribute their best endeavors to promote the internal trade, manufactures and population of their country, by facilitating every possible communication between the different parts of the state, have lately formed themselves into a society, by the name above mentioned. And knowing that the Legislature, with the laudable intention of advancing the best interests of this commonwealth, and availing themselves of the extensive information, which they have obtained of the geography and situation of the country, have now under their consideration the important subject of roads and inland navigation; we, therefore, beg leave, with all possible deference, to suggest some important considerations which have occurred to us in our enquiries into this subject.

Pennsylvania, from her situation, and extent of territory, is a respectable commonwealth in the Union. Her soil is fertile, her products various, and her rivers, by the bountiful Author of Nature, have been made to flow in every direction, as if on purpose to bear from all parts the wealth and produce of the land, in an easy, cheap and expeditious manner, to her principal mart and port in the city of Philadelphia. To combine the interests of all the parts of the state, and to cement them in a perpetual commercial and political union, by the improvement of those natural advantages, is one of the greatest works which can be submitted to *legislative* wisdom; and the present moment is particularly auspicious for the undertaking, and if neglected, the loss will be hard to retrieve.

When once our trade hath forced its way, even through a less advantageous channel, it is difficult to alter its course; and a little expense, judiciously and seasonably applied, may retain a stream in its channel, which with immense sums cannot be restored, if once diverted from it. Large emigrations from Europe are now directing their course to this country, and will be encouraged by every improvement we make, by means of roads and water communications with the distant parts of the state. The constant influx of settlers from the eastern states is also a considerable object. Being stopped, for the present, by the Indian disturbances from swarming into the western territory, many of them may be encouraged to make a halt or settlement in this state, if they find good roads and communications in the different parts thereof.

It may be proper, therefore, before we proceed farther, to subjoin a general statement of the various communications and improvements of which Pennsylvania is capable in this way; so far as relates to navigation.

DELAWARE NAVIGATION

From the tide water at Trenton falls to lake Otsego, the head of the north-east branch of Susquehanna.

No. I.

	Miles.	Ch.	Total.	
From Trenton falls to the mouth of Lehigh at Easton,	50	15	50	15
To Lechewaeksin branch of Delaware,	94	12	144	27
Thence to *Stockport* on Delaware, a little below the junction of the Mohock and Popachton branches,	66	24	210	51
Portage from Stockport to Harmony, at the great Bend,	20	00	230	51
Thence up the north east branch of Susquehanna to Otsego lake,	70	00	300	51

No. II.

From the tide water on Delaware to Oswego on lake Ontario.

	Miles	Ch	Total	
To Harmony, at the great Bend of Susquehanna, as above,	230	51	230	51
Down Susquehanna to the mouth of Tioga,	65	00	295	51
Up Tioga to Newtown,	18	00	313	51
Portage to Connedessago lake, which may be turned wholly into lock navigation by Newtown creek,	18	00	331	51
Down Connedessago lake,	36	00	367	51
Down Seneca or Onandago river to Oswego,	86	00	453	51

Estimate of the expense of opening this navigation, from Trenton falls to Stockport, near the state line.

From Trenton falls to the mouth of Lehigh,	£. 1005
From Lehigh or *Easton*, to Stockport,	1243
Portage from Stockport to Harmony at £.20 per mile,	400
	£. 2648

SUSQUEHANNA

SUSQUEHANNA NAVIGATION,

As connected with Schuylkill on the east, and Ohio and the great lakes on the west.

No. I.

From Philadelphia, or the tide waters of Schuylkill, to Pittsburgh on the Ohio.

	Miles.	Ch.	Total.	
Up Schuylkill to the mouth of Tulpehocken,	61	00	61	00
Thence up Tulpehocken to the end of the proposed canal,	37	09	98	09
Length of the canal,	4	15	102	24
Down Quitipahilla to Swatara,	15	20	117	44
Down Swatara to Susquehanna,	23	00	140	44
Up Susquehanna to Juniata,	23	28	163	72
Up Juniata to Huntingdon,	86	12	250	04
From Huntingdon, on Juniata, to the mouth of Poplar run,	42	00	292	04
Portage to the Canoe Place on Conemaugh,	18	00	310	04
Down Conemaugh to Old Town at the mouth of Stoney Creek,	18	00	328	04
Down Conemaugh and Kiskeminetas to Allegheny,	69	00	397	04
Down Allegheny river to *Pittsburgh* on the *Ohio*,	29	00	426	04

Estimate of the expense of clearing this navigation, from Philadelphia to Pittsburgh.

	£	
Schuylkill from the tide water to Reading, by David Rittenhouse and others,	1147	0
By Benjamin Rittenhouse and John Adlum,	1519	13
Clearing the Tulpehocken, by ditto,	1419	9
The canal from Tulpehocken to Quitipahilla, 20 feet wide and 7 feet deep on an average,*		
The Quitipahilla and Swatara,	18900	0
Susquehanna from Swatara to Juniata,	300	0
The Juniata to Frank's Town,	2320	0
Canal or lock navigation to Poplar run (if found necessary, which probably will not be the case)	7000	0
Portage of 18 miles to Conemaugh at £.20 per mile,	360	0
Conemaugh and Kiskeminetas to Allegheny,	7150	0
Total expense from Philadelphia to Pittsburgh, being four hundred and twenty-six miles,		

* N. B. The Society have left a blank for the estimate of the canal, as they mean to enquire further whether it cannot be done cheaper upon a plan of lock navigation.

(4)

No. II.

From Philadelphia to Presqu' Isle on lake Erie, by the Juniata and Kiskeminetas, &c.

	Miles. Ch.	Total.
To the mouth of Kiskeminetas, by the same route, as above,	397 04	397 04
Up the Allegheny to French creek,	83 43	480 47
Up French creek to Le Bœuf,	65 40	546 07
Portage from Le Bœuf to Presqu' Isle,	15 40	561 47

N. B. The sum of £.500 for French creek, and £.400 for the portage, is all the additional expense in the navigation from Kiskeminetas to Presqu' Isle, or the lakes.

No. III.

From Philadelphia to Presqu' Isle, by the west branch of Susquehanna, Sinnemahoning and Conewango.

	Miles. Ch.	Total.
From Philadelphia to Swatara, as above,	140 44	140 44
Up Susquehanna to the west branch, at Sunbury,	65 00	205 44
Up the west branch to the mouth of Sinnemahoning,	106 00	311 44
Up Sinnemahoning to the Forks,	15 20	326 64
Up the north branch of Sinnemahoning,	19 40	346 24
By the portage to the head of Allegheny river,	23 00	369 24
Down Allegheny river (partly through New York state) to the mouth of Conewango,	76 00	445 24
Up Conewango to New York line 11 miles—thence up the same through the state of New York 17 miles to Chatuaghque lake,	28 00	473 24
Across Chatuaghque lake to its head,	17 00	490 24
Portage to lake Erie at the mouth of Chatuaghque creek,	9 20	499 44
Along lake Erie to Presqu' Isle,	25 00	524 44

No. IV.

From Philadelphia to Presqu' Isle, by the west branch of Susquehanna, Sinnemahoning and Toby's creek.

	Miles. Ch.	Total.
From Philadelphia to the forks of Sinnemahoning, as before,	326 64	326 64
Up the west branch of Sinnemahoning,	24 00	350 64
Portage to little Toby's creek,	14 00	364 64
Down little Toby's creek to the main branch,	10 00	374 64
Down the main branch of Toby's creek to the Allegheny,	70 00	444 64
Up the Allegheny to French creek,	35 00	479 64
Up French creek and the Portage to Presqu' Isle,	81 00	560 64

No. V.

From the tide waters of Susquehanna to Pittsburgh. M... C. Tot.

From Thomas's near Susquehanna ferry, to the mouth of Swatara,	54 00	54 00
From the mouth of Swatara, as above, to Pittsburgh, -	285 40	339 40

No. VI.

From the tide waters of Potomack, at George Town, to Pittsburgh.

From George Town to William's Port at the mouth of Conecocheaque, - - - - - -	98 15	98 15
From William's Port to Fort Cumberland, - -	93 36	191 51
From Fort Cumberland to the mouth of Savage river, -	30 44	222 15
Portage from the mouth of Savage river on Potomack to Dunkard Bottom on Cheat river, - - - -	37 20	259 35
Down Cheat river to Monongahela, - - -	25 00	284 35
Down Monongahela to Pittsburgh, - - -	102 00	386 35

No. VII.

From Conedessago lake to New York.

From Geneva, at the outlet of Conedessago lake, by Seneca river to the Three Rivers, - - - -	62 00	62 00
To the Oneida lake, - - - -	28 00	90 00
Up the Oneida lake to Wood creek, - -	18 00	108 00
By Wood creek (a very crooked course, 25 miles, but supposed longer)	30 00	138 00
Portage to the Mohock river, - - -	1 00	139 00
To the rapids or falls of the Mohock river, - -	60 00	199 00
Portage, - - - - - -	1 00	200 00
Down the Mohock river to Schenectady, - -	55 00	255 00
Portage to Albany, - - - -	15 00	270 00
By Hudson's river to New York, - -	165 00	435 00

No. VIII.

From the middle of the Genessee country to New York.

Down Genessee river to lake Ontario, - -	30 00	30 00
Along lake Ontario to Oswego, - - -	60 00	90 00
From Oswego to the Three Rivers, - -	24 00	114 00
From thence to New York, as above, - -	373 00	487 00

No. IX.

	Miles. Ch.	Total.
From the Conedeſſago lake by the Portage, and by Tioga and Suſquehanna to the mouth of Swatara,	260 00	260 00
Thence to Philadelphia, as above,	140 00	401 00

No. X.

	Miles. Ch.	Total.
From Conedeſſago by Tioga and Suſquehanna to the great Bend,	101 00	101 00
The Portage to Stockport and down Delaware to tide water,	230 51	331 51
To Philadelphia,	34 00	365 51

On the inſpection of the map hereunto annexed, compared with the foregoing ſtatement of diſtances and water communications, as they may be improved to connect the weſtern waters of the Suſquehanna, the Ohio and great lakes, with the port of Philadelphia; an almoſt unbounded proſpect of future *wealth* and importance opens to the citizens of this commonwealth. That this ſubject may be better comprehended in detail, give us leave to conſider it under two great heads.

Firſt, The *Delaware navigation*, as ſtated in No. I. and II. by which the countries on the waters of the north eaſt branch of Suſquehanna up to its head at lake Otſego, and all the countries lying from the mouth of Tioga to lake Ontario, may be connected with the city of Philadelphia; having only twenty miles portage from Stockport on Delaware to Harmony at the great bend of Suſquehanna, in the whole diſtance of three hundred miles and an half from the tide water of Delaware to lake Otſego; and only eighteen miles more in the much larger diſtance of four hundred and fifty-three miles and an half from the ſame tide waters to Oſwego on lake Ontario.

The expenſe of this whole navigation, by the eſtimate annexed, is only—
For the river Delaware, - - - - - - £. 2242 0
The portage of twenty miles, - - - - 400 0
And the Tioga waters and portage, about - -

But as the Tioga waters, and the communications from thence to lake Ontario, lie within the ſtate of New York, it is probable that they will not be improved by that ſtate, unleſs it can be done with a view to draw the trade of that country by the Oneida lake, Wood creek, &c. into Hudſon's river, and even when that ſhall happen, by a happy rivalſhip between the cities of Philadelphia and New York, to draw the trade of thoſe vaſt countries to their reſpective ports, a great part of it will come with more eaſe to the former than to the latter; and while the waters are left in their preſent unimproved ſtate, every advantage is on the ſide of Pennſylvania, by means of the navigation down the *Tioga*, and then either down Suſquehanna to the mouth of Swatara, and thence to Philadelphia by the waters of Swatara, Quitipahilla, Tulpehocken and Schuylkill; or from the mouth of Tioga up Suſquehanna to the great bend, and thence by the portage to Stockport, and by Delaware to Philadelphia. Taking Conedeſſago lake as a central place of embarkation for the ſettlers in the Geneſſee country, the diſtance

tance to the city of New York will be four hundred and thirty-five miles (See No. VII.) whereof seventeen miles are land carriage; and the diſtance to Philadelphia, by Delaware (See No. II.) will be three hundred and thirty-one miles; or by Swatara and Schuylkill (See No. IX.) will be four hundred and one miles. Or if the middle of the Geneſſee ſettlement, on the Geneſſee river, be taken as the place of beginning, the diſtance to New York will be four hundred and eighty-ſeven miles, whereof * ſeventeen miles are land carriage, (See No. VIII.) and the diſtance to Philadelphia three hundred and ſixty-five miles and an half (See No. X.) whereof thirty-eight miles are land carriage.

Connected with the Delaware navigation, we beg leave further to add, that above Stockport, the Mohock and Popaughton branches, are each navigable for boats of fifteen tons for more than fifty miles above their junction, and conſiderably higher ſtill for rafts. The Lehigh and Lechawackſen, likewiſe, offer themſelves as very important branches of this navigation, lying in the interior parts of the ſtate; but nothing need be added to the report of the Commiſſioners on this head. We proceed, therefore, to the ſecond great and moſt important head, viz.

The *Suſquehanna navigation*, as it may be connected with the Schuylkill waters, on the one hand, and the Ohio waters and great lakes on the other. Here is a navigation which we may properly call our own, paſſing through the moſt inhabited and central parts of the ſtate; in which we can have no rivals, if duly improved, and opening ſuch numerous ſources and channels of inland trade, all leading to the port of Philadelphia, as perhaps no other nation or ſea port on the whole globe can boaſt of.

For, in the firſt place, if we turn our view to the immenſe territories connected with the Ohio and Miſſiſſippi waters, and bordering on the great lakes, it will appear from the tables of diſtances, that our communication with thoſe vaſt countries (conſidering Fort Pitt as the port of entrance upon them) is as eaſy and may be rendered as cheap, as to any other port on the Atlantic tide waters. The diſtance from Philadelphia to the Allegheny, at the mouth of Kiſkeminetas, is nearly the ſame as from the mouth of Monongahela to George Town on Potomack; and ſuppoſing the computed diſtances from Pittſburgh to the Dunkard Bottom to be juſt, and the navigation of Cheat river, on the one hand, and the Potomack, at the mouth of Savage river, on the other, to be, at all ſeaſons of the year, equal to the navigation of the Kiſkeminetas, Conemaugh and Juniata; yet as the portage from Dunkard Bottom to the Potomack, at the mouth of Savage river, is thirty-ſeven miles and a quarter, and the portage from Conemaugh to Juniata only eighteen miles (which may be conſiderably ſhortened by locks) there can be no doubt but that the tranſportation of all kinds of goods and merchandize from Philadelphia to Pittſburgh may be at a much cheaper rate than from any other ſea port on the Atlantic waters.

This is not mentioned with a view to diſparage the internal navigation of our ſiſter ſtates, more eſpecially *Maryland* and *Virginia*. We admire their noble exertions to improve the natural advantages of their country, and deſire to imitate and to emulate them.

* In this route to New York there are the ſame portages, viz. ſeventeen miles, as in the other from the Conedaſſago lake, ſuppoſing Geneſſee river could be made navigable; but it is doubtful whether it can be made uſeful in navigation, having many falls, and one of them ſixty feet.

them. Every improvement, and every new communication with the western territories, promoted by any of the United States, by which the trade of the lakes, the Ohio and the Miſſiſſippi waters can be drawn to our ſea ports, is a benefit to the whole Union. By no other methods than by opening eaſy communications, both by good roads and ſafe water carriage, can the ſettlers, in thoſe vaſt weſtern countries, be made uſeful to the Atlantic ſtates, and comfortable in their own ſituation. Nor can we expect by any other means than by inviting their trade, and making it their intereſt to be connected with us, that we can long ſecure ſuch connection. But, although a conſiderable part of the ſettlers on the Ohio waters may be accommodated by the Potomack navigation, and the ſtate of Pennſylvania may only have a ſhare in the trade of thoſe waters; yet there remains to us the immenſe trade of the lakes, taking Preſqu' Iſle, which is within our own ſtate, as the great mart or place of embarkaation. Here there can be no competition, in reſpect to the diſtances or the eaſe of water carriage, between the port of Philadelphia and any other port on the Atlantic tide waters; whichſoever of the three communications, between Philadelphia and Preſqu' Iſle, we may chooſe to purſue.

Of thoſe three communications, it is of importance to chooſe the beſt in the firſt inſtance, and not to neglect the improvement of it; nor to entertain doubts and delays, till the opportunity of receiving benefit from it be entirely loſt, and the trade of thoſe vaſt countries drawn into other channels.

We ſhall ſpeak firſt of the communication with Preſqu' Iſle, by the Chadaghque lake, the Conewango river, part of Allegheny, the Sinnemahoning, Suſquehanna, Swatara and Schuylkill (No. III.) which appears to be the ſhorteſt, being about five hundred and twenty-four miles and an half. The navigation of the Conewango and north branch of Sinnemahoning, according to the report of the Commiſſioners, may be made very good, and is, on that account, as well as the ſhortneſs of the diſtance, preferable to that by the way of Toby's creek and the weſt branch of Sinnemahoning. But a conſiderable part of this communication lies through the ſtate of New York, in a yet unſettled country; and although it leads, in the moſt direct way to Preſqu' Iſle and the great lakes, it cannot be of any great uſe in the main communication with the Ohio and Miſſiſſippi by the way of Pittſburgh, which is the great object of preſent conſideration.

The ſecond route from Philadelphia to Preſqu' Iſle, by the weſt branch of Suſquehanna, as connected with Swatara and Schuylkill, and by the Sinnemahoning and Toby's creek, being five hundred and ſixty miles and a quarter (See No. IV.) paſſes indeed wholly through our own ſtate; but beſides what has been already mentioned concerning the waters of Toby's creek, compared with the Conewango and Chadaghque lake, this navigation could be of no farther uſe than the former, in reſpect to the main communication with Pittſburgh, as the mouth of Toby's creek lies fifty miles higher on the Allegheny than the mouth of Kiſkeminetas; and even with reſpect to Preſqu' Iſle, the navigation from Philadelphia, by the way of the Juniata and Kiſkeminetas, is as ſhort as by the way of Toby's creek, the latter being five hundred and ſixty miles and three quarters, as mentioned above, and the former five hundred and ſixty-one miles and an half.

Third, This third communication, then, is that which embraces all prefent interefts. It connects Philadelphia with Pittfburgh and all the Ohio waters, by the Schuylkill, the Swatara and Juniata branches of Sufquehanna, and the Kifkeminetas branch of Allegheny, with the diftance of five hundred and fixty-one miles and an half (No. II.) and alfo Philadelphia and Prefqu' Ifle, ufing the fame waters, as above, to the mouth of Kifkeminetas, and then by the eafy waters of Allegheny and French creek. In this whole communication to Pittfburgh, there are only eighteen miles portage between the Juniata and Conemaugh (which may be confiderably reduced as is faid before) and only the addition of fifteen miles and an half more at the portage from Le Bœuf to Prefqu' Ifle, which portage is, likewife, included in both the other communications. In this ftatement of portages, it is fuppofed that the canal or lock navigation between the heads of Tulpehocken and Quitipahilla, is to be compleated; but if that work fhould be thought too great to begin with, it will be only the addition of four miles portage, by an excellent and level road.

The navigation, by this route, we beg leave to recommend to the Legiflature, as one of the firft and greateft works which they can undertake for the honor and advantage of their country. It is a work within their reach—a work in which not only the citizens of this ftate, but of the United States in general, are deeply interefted. The expenfe, even including the canal, has been eftimated, and doth not exceed the fum which would be requifite to compleat a good road of fifty or fixty miles in fome of the interior parts of the ftate, and which, after all, would only be of *partial* benefit, contributing but little to unite the remote parts of the fame, in one eafy central chain of communication, with the capital.

The improvement of roads is, however, one great part of the defign of our *affociation*, and we mean to make it our endeavor to bring forward and to encourage ufeful plans for this purpofe. Some roads, as connected with the plan of inland navigation, require the immediate attention of the Legiflature. Among thefe are the different portages mentioned in the refpective water communications ftated above; and, particularly, that between Stockport on Delaware, and Harmony, at the great bend of Sufquehanna, and between the mouth of the Poplar run on Juniata, and the Canoe Place on Conemaugh. Another moft important road, as connected with the navigation fcheme, will be from the higheft boatable waters of Yohiogeny, near the Turkey Foot, to the junction of the Rays-town branch of Juniata and Dunning's creek near Bedford; or even to the mouth of Poplar run on the Frank's-town branch. By this road, all the inhabitants of the upper parts of Wafhington and Fayette counties, and part of Bedford county, would have accefs to the great water communication by the Juniata, or to the great *ftate road* from Bedford to Philadelphia; avoiding the mountainous and circuitous courfe they are now obliged to purfue; and a great part of their trade, which would otherwife go to Potomack, would be thereby fecured to Pennfylvania.

In this view, alfo, the ftate road, through Lancafter, Carlifle and Bedford to Pittfburgh, is an object of primary confideration, and may be undertaken without delay or injury to the plan of weftern navigation. This commonwealth, we are happy to believe, is now, in its resources, equal to the accomplishment of all necessary improvement, both of roads and navigation.

We would beg leave, before we conclude, to point out some other roads as worthy of attention, viz.

I. The road through Reading and Sunbury, and thence to be continued by the best and most practicable route to Presqu' Isle, or the lands on French creek.

II. The road through Bethlehem to the northern boundary of the state, at some point between Delaware and the great bend of Susquehanna.

III. A road leading from Hudson's river, in the state of New York, to be continued from Stockport on Delaware, across towards the west branch of Susquehanna, between Munsey and the great Island, and to join the road, mentioned above, as leading to French creek and Presqu' Isle.

But, in every view, we humbly conceive, that the laying out and improving those roads ought not to interfere with, or delay the improvement of our inland navigation. The ease and cheapness of water carriage, compared with every other, furnish sufficient arguments, on this subject, if there were none else.

The annexed comparative view, of the expenses of both, is submitted to the consideration of the Legislature, as a conclusion to this memorial.

Signed on behalf, and by order of the Society,

ROBERT MORRIS, *President.*

February 7th. 1791.

Remarks

Remarks and Calculations respecting the Communications between Schuylkill and Susquehanna.

IN the present year 1790, by the best estimates that can be obtained the quantity of one hundred and fifty thousand bushels of grain has been brought down the Susquehanna, and passed through Middle Town, on its way to Philadelphia market. Juniata has afforded a very considerable part of this quantity; and here it must be observed, that the lands on this river are but in an infant state of cultivation, and suppose them to be ever so well improved, the proportion they bear to the lands on the other branches of the Susquehanna is not more than one-fifth part.

In the year 1788, large quantities of wheat and flour were carried up the river for the use of the settlers in Northumberland county: since last March, about thirty thousand bushels of wheat returned down the stream to market from said county. It may also be reasonably expected, that should an easy inland communication be effected between the Susquehanna and the Schuylkill, the whole produce of Cumberland, and part of York county, would cross the Susquehanna to the Philadelphia market. From these principles it is evident, that there will be an annual increase of the country produce that will descend the Susquehanna, although, from so short an experience, certainty in our estimates cannot be expected: but, in order to reduce the subject more to view, let the annual increase be put at one-eighth, which I expect will be allowed, on all hands, to be guarded by moderation and justified by strong probability.

I said one hundred and fifty thousand bushels of grain are allowed to have passed to Middle Town in the present year, which, augmented by an annual increase of one-eighth, will, in 1793, amount to two hundred and six thousand two hundred and fifty bushels, which, at two shillings and six pence per bushel, (the carriage, on the present principles, to the Philadelphia market) amounts to twenty-five thousand seven hundred and eighty-one pounds, five shillings; then, by adding one-eighth, the annual increase, it will stand thus:—

£.	s.	d.			year
25,781	5	0	for the		1793
28,125	0	0	-	-	1794
30,468	15	0	-	-	1795
32,812	10	0	-	-	1796
35,156	5	0	-	-	1797
37,500	0	0	-	-	1798
39,843	15	0	-	-	1799
42,187	10	0	-	-	1800
£. 271,875	0	0	Whole amount of carriage to market.		

The abovementioned quantity of grain is equal to five thousand five hundred and twenty-four tons and an half; and suppose one-third of the weight is carried back, in salt, liquors and other merchandize, at five shillings per hundred or five pounds per ton, there will be one thousand eight hundred and forty-two tons, with an annual increase of one hundred and sixty-seven tons.—It will then stand thus:—

£.	s.	d.			
9,210	0	0	for the year	1793
10,045	0	0	- -	1794
10,880	0	0	- -	1795
11,715	0	0	- -	1796
12,550	0	0	- -	1797
13,385	0	0	- -	1798
14,220	0	0	- -	1799
15,055	0	0	- -	1800

£. 97,060 0 0 Whole amount of back carriage in eight years.

The whole amount of carriage to and from Middle Town in eight years:—

    To Philadelphia, £. 271,875
     Middle Town, 97,060

      £. 368,935

Suppose the quantities before mentioned to be carried by water, the wheat at one shilling and six pence per bushel, and the back loads at three shillings per hundred or three pounds per ton, it will then stand thus:—

To this market, £.				for the year	From this market, £.			
15,468	15	0		1793	5,426	0	0
16,875	0	0	- -	1794	- - -	5,927	0	0
18,281	5	0	- -	1795	- - -	6,428	0	0
19,687	10	0	- -	1796	- - -	6,929	0	0
21,093	15	0	- -	1797	- - -	7,430	0	0
22,500	0	0	- -	1798	- - -	7,931	0	0
23,906	5	0	- -	1799	- - -	8,432	0	0
25,312	10	0	- -	1800	- - -	8,933	0	0

£. 163,125 0 0   £. 57,436 0 0
 57,436 0 0

£. 220,561 0 0 Whole amount of carriage by water.

   Carriage by land in eight years, £. 368,935
   Ditto by water,   -   -   220,561

      Balance, £. 148,374

A number of observations naturally present themselves as consequences of this water communication: First, The difference between the carriage by land and that by water, during the aforesaid period, is one hundred and forty-eight thousand three hundred and seventy-four pounds, which will be a clear gain to the country, and the stock now vested in horses, waggons, &c. could be employed to other useful purposes; the so general use of horses might be abated and oxen used in their stead by the farmers, whose principal reason for giving so decided a preference to horses is their being supposed better for draught on the roads: a more general use of oxen would not only be attended with immediate profit to the husbandman, but would tend to increase the article of beef as an export. The lands in the old counties, below the mountains, are known to have abated in that virgin fertility which attends all new cultivation;—they must now be manured. Added to this, the population is increasing very rapidly; the operation of these causes, in a few years more, will make the consumption equal to the produce in the old counties. If the staple of the port of Philadelphia is to be supported, it can be best done by conducting the streams of commerce, in the article of grain, from the Susquehanna to this city.

The late information obtained from the commissioners who have viewed the communications with the Allegheny and lake Erie, make it highly probable, that an immense trade will one day be carried on from Philadelphia with the great lakes and furr countries, and with the settlements on the Ohio, &c. The proposed communication between Schuylkill and Susquehanna will serve as a basis to this traffick, whether the route be by the Juniata or the other branches of the Susquehanna.

The expense attending the transportation of two hundred and six thousand two hundred and fifty bushels of grain to market.

THE above quantity of grain is equal to five thousand five hundred and twenty-four tons and an half, and, a boat to carry six tons, will be equal to nine hundred and twenty-one boat loads, and each boat to pass and repass eight times, annually, it will take one hundred and fifteen boats to transport the quantity above mentioned in a season;—the expense of hands and provisions attending each load will be fifteen pounds—consequently, nine hundred and twenty one loads will cost thirteen thousand eight hundred and fifteen pounds, and the annual increase of expenses for an additional number of boats, hands, &c. to transport the increase of produce, will be one thousand five hundred and twenty pounds a year, and then it will stand thus:—

For the year 1793   £. 13,815 0 0
            1794   15,335 0 0
            1795   16,855 0 0
            1796   18,375 0 0
            1797   19,895 0 0
            1798   21,415 0 0
            1799   22,935 0 0
            1800   24,455 0 0
                     £. 153,080 0 0

The whole expense of carriage, and for seventy-seven additional boats, some of which will be seven-eighths worn, and so on to one-eighth, allowing a boat to last eight years.

Amount

(14)

Amount of carriage by water in eight years, £. 220,561
Expenfe attending the fame, - - 153,080

Balance, £. 67,481

It is fuppofed, by thefe calculations, that the boats for the beginning of the carriage, will be taken in the eftimate with the canal.

The grain confumed as horfe-feed will be another object of attention:—two hundred and fix thoufand two hundred and fifty bufhels of grain, at forty-five to a waggon load, are equal to four thoufand five hundred and eighty-three loads; each team, to be ten days on the road, will eat ten bufhels of rye, which is equal to forty-five thoufand eight hundred and thirty bufhels, which, with the annual increafe, will, in eight years, amount to four hundred and eighty-three thoufand four hundred and eighty bufhels; or, annually, it will ftand thus:—

For 1793	-	45,840
1794	- -	50,010
1795	-	54,180
1796	- -	58,350
1797	-	62,520
1798	- -	66,690
1799	-	70,860
1800	- -	75,030

483,840 bufhels.

Eftimate of the expenfe of clearing the river Schuylkill, from the falls to Reading, by David Rittenhoufe and others, in the year 1773.

Clearing the Schuylkill from the falls to the Spring
Mill, - - - - - £. 192 0 0
Ditto to Reading, - - - - 955 0 0
———————
£. 1147 0 0

Eftimate of the expenfe of clearing the river Schuylkill, from the falls to Reading, by Benjamin Rittenhoufe and John Adlum, in 1789.

Clearing the Schuylkill from the falls to the Spring
Mill, - - - - £. 270 0 0
Ditto to Reading, - - - 1111 10 0
Contingencies, £. 10 per cent. - - 138 3 0
———————
Sum carried over £. 1519 13 0

Sum brought forward, £. 1519 13 0

Estimate of the expense of clearing the Tulpehocken creek from its mouth to the head of the same, by Benjamin Rittenhouse and John Adlum.

Clearing the Tulpehocken from its mouth to Lechner's mill, twenty-eight miles and sixteen chains up said stream,	£. 1289 10 0	
Contingent expenses, say ten per cent.	129 19 0	
Amount of the estimate from Lechner's mill to the mouth of the creek,		£. 1419 9 0
A canal to be cut from Lechner's mill to Loy's spring at the head of the Tulpehocken creek, about seven miles and a half in length, suppose twenty feet wide, and, on an average, seven feet deep, the expense of common cutting at nine pence per yard,	£. 7699 19 9	
For ten locks in the above distance,	2000 0 0	
For temporary damages to lands, impediments to works, &c. suppose ten per cent. on the above,	970 0 0	
Amount of expense from Lechner's mill to the head of Tulpehocken creek,		£. 10,669 19 9
For cutting the canal from Loy's spring, the head of Tulpehocken creek, to Kucher's dam on the head of the Quitapahilla creek, four miles and sixty perches, on an average twenty-five feet deep and thirty feet wide, the expense of common cutting nine pence per yard,		£. 23,031 4 6
The amount of the expense for clearing the Schuylkill, Tulpehocken canal, &c. to the head of the Quitapahilla,		£. 36,640 6 3

N. B. This expense may be avoided by leaving a portage of about four miles, which will reduce the whole to £. 32,540.

Amount of expense on Quitapahilla and Swatara to Susquehanna, by Matlack, Maclay and Adlum, in 1790,		£. 18,900 0 0
Amount of expense from Philadelphia to Susquehanna by way of Schuylkill and Swatara,		£. 55,540 6 3
From the mouth of Swatara up the Susquehanna to the mouth of Juniata, by Galbreath, Boyd and Huling,		300 0 0

Sum carried over, £. 55,840 6 3

Sum brought forward, £.55,840	6	3
Up Juniata to Water-street on the Frank's Town branch of Juniata, 820	0	0
Clearing the Frank's Town branch to Frank's Old Town, by Matlack, Maclay and Adlum, 1500	0	0
Canal from thence to Poplar run, 7000	0	0
Portage to Little Conemaugh, eighteen miles, at £.20 per mile, 360	0	0
From the Canoe Place on the Little Conemaugh, down the same and Kiskeminetas to Allegheny, 7150	0	0
Opening French creek to Le Bœuf, 500	0	0
Road from Le Bœuf to Presqu' Isle, 400	0	0
Contingencies in Matlack's, Maclay's and Adlum's estimate, 3,599	0	0
Amount of expense from Philadelphia to Presqu' Isle on lake Erie, by way of Schuylkill, Swatara, Juniata, &c. £.77,169	6	3

N. B. This may be reduced to £.54,169 by leaving a portage of four miles between the Tulpehocken and Quitapahilla.

Estimate of the expense for opening the navigation and communications to Presqu' Isle, on lake Erie, from Philadelphia, by way of Schuylkill, Swatara, the west branch of Susquehanna, Sinemahoning, Conewango, &c.

From Philadelphia to the mouth of Swatara, by Schuylkill, &c. £.55,540	6	3
From Swatara to North Town at the forks of Susquehanna, 600	0	0
To the Canoe Place on Sinemahoning, 660	0	0
Portage to the Allegheny, 460	0	0
From the head of the Allegheny to the mouth of Chataughque creek on lake Erie, 1400	0	0
Whole amount of expense to Presqu' Isle as above, £.58,660	6	3

N. B. This estimate may be reduced to £.35,660 by leaving the distance between Tulpehocken and Quitapahilla a portage.

Estimate of the expense of opening the river Delaware, from the falls, at Trenton, to Stockport, near the Popachton branch of the same, and the portage across to Harmony on the great bend of Susquehanna.

From the Falls at Trenton to Easton, £.1005	0	0
From thence to Stockport, 1243	0	0
Portage to the great bend on the north-east branch of Susquehanna, 400	0	0
Amount, £.2648	0	0

A

A proposal and plan for carrying into immediate execution the improvement of roads and inland navigation.

To the Senate and House of Representatives of the commonwealth of Pennsylvania, in General Assembly met.

THE Society for promoting the improvement of roads and inland navigation, beg leave to present the result of their enquiries, concerning the best method, and most effectual plan, for the carrying that important work into immediate execution. And, in the first place, with respect to the improvement of roads, on turning our attention to the history of this work, as it hath been conducted in other countries, and especially in the island of Great Britain, we find that but little attention was paid to the improvement of roads, till in the year 1285, the first statute was passed for widening the roads between market towns in "England," but this was done purely to prevent robberies, and not the least hint of its being yet necessary for the use of carriages or to promote commerce. But, in the year 1555, a statute was passed " taking notice that the high ways were become very noisome and tedious to travel, and dangerous to all passengers and carriages;" wherefore, it was enacted, " That every parish should annually choose two Surveyors of the high ways, to see that the parishioners, according to their lands, abilities and farms, shall send their carts, horses, men, tools, &c. four days in every year, for mending the roads, &c." and, from this time, to the reign of Charles II. there were no less than twenty six statutes, on similar principles, passed for keeping the highways in repair; from which the road laws of Pennsylvania have been in great measure copied, only substituting townships for parishes. But soon after the restoration of Charles II. we find it set forth, " That the vast increase of the capital city of London, and of the nation's commerce and manufactures, with the concomitant increase of wealth and luxury, had introduced such numbers of heavy wheel carriages on the roads, as rendered it impracticable, in most cases, for parishes to keep their own part of the roads in repair; more especially in the counties lying nearer London, and in the manufacturing counties; and, therefore, a more *equitable* and *effectual* method was introduced of tolls and toll-gates called turnpikes; by which means the burden of putting and keeping the roads in repair (as it is strongly expressed) was put upon the *identical wearers-out of the roads*, according to the use they made of them—and, accordingly, upon this *new* and more *equitable* and *effectual plan*, many *local*, as well as *general*, statutes have been enacted for limiting the weight of waggon loads, the breadth of wheel rims, called fellies; the number of horses, &c. And what has been said of roads may be applied to the deepening of rivers, and the improvement of inland navigation, by locks, tolls, and canals," which was begun about the same time, and is now extended over the whole kingdom by subsequent acts of parliament *special* and *local* as well as more general.

E The

(18)

The present circumstances of Pennsylvania, in respect to the increase of commerce, wheel carriages, &c. and the unimproved state of our roads and inland navigable waters, being so similar to those of England in the time of Charles II. the foregoing reasoning will justify the conclusion which we mean to draw from it, namely—That the putting or keeping the great roads in repair, either in the counties near the capital city of Philadelphia, or, indeed, in distant counties but thinly inhabited, would be a burthen not only intolerable to the inhabitants of the particular townships, through which the roads pass, but, likewise, *unequal* in itself, and ought neither to be borne by the state at large, nor yet by the particular townships and counties, but, for the greater part, " by the *identical wearers-out* of the roads," according to the use they make of them.—And the like reasoning applies to the improvement of rivers and opening of canals for water carriage.

From these preliminary observations, the Society beg leave to lay down the following principles, as the ground work of the *plan* herewith submitted to the consideration of the Legislature of Pennsylvania.

First, The method of turnpike roads and toll navigation must be adopted.

Secondly, The work, both of roads and navigation, must be undertaken and carried into execution, by separate companies and associations of men; upon some uniform and consistent plan, aided and directed by the Legislature; as neither the state alone, nor any number of companies without public regulations and assistance, can be adequate to the great work in all its parts; and, therefore, the assistance of the state should be apportioned to different parts of the work, with a *liberal* and *equal hand*, in respect both to *roads* and *navigation*, as it may be most necessary, and where the smallness of the tolls, the distance from the *market* and other circumstances may yield the least probability of an adequate encouragement or speedy reimbursement to the adventurers.

Upon those principles, the Society beg leave to offer the following

Heads of a Plan:—

I. The Legislature to appropriate a sum not less than   dollars to this object.

II. In order that there may be sufficient wisdom, consistency, experience, impartiality and public spirit attached to the execution of the work, and interested in its success; the Legislature to appoint, by law, a " Board of Commissioners for the improvements of roads and inland navigation, within the state of Pennsylvania."

III. The Board to consist of   members, of which the Governor shall be President, with a Vice-President, to be annually elected. They shall meet once a week, or as often as may be needful. The time and place of every meeting to be announced in one of the daily news-papers, and the members present, being not less than   to be capable of transacting business.

IV.

IV. The Board of Commissioners to be allowed the use of a room, or rooms, in some of the public buildings in the city of Philadelphia; wherein they may hold their meetings, and deposit their books, maps, plans, and other papers. They are to be allowed firing, candles, stationary, clerks' hire and actual contingent necessary expenses to be paid by the public. But *they shall not receive any pay* for their own time or personal services, unless when any of them shall be employed by the Board to make surveys, or to inspect or superintend any of the works that may be carried on under their direction; in which cases they shall be entitled to their travelling charges and expenses.

V. The general and standing powers of the said Board of Commissioners shall be as follow, *viz.*

1. To employ, at the public expense, a proper person or persons, to examine, survey, mark out, and report, in writing, such roads as may be deemed the most proper to be established as turnpikes, assigning their reasons that induced them to be of opinion, in any instance, that it will be of public utility to depart from the present or old line of any established road.

2. To determine finally (after considering such reports and obtaining all necessary information) upon the line of road, which shall be established as turnpike.

3. To determine on such roads as, not being suitable for turnpike, ought to be made or repaired at public cost, and to employ proper persons to perform the same.

4. To advertise the roads which they shall establish for turnpikes; receive propositions and enter into contracts with individuals, companies or corporations, for constructing and mending the said roads, in such manner, and upon such principles, as have, in other countries, been found upon experience to be best.

5. To fix in each contract, the particular road, and the extent or length thereof which the parties are to improve, and the rates or tolls which they shall be entitled to receive for horses, cattle, carriages, &c.

6. To appoint a superintendant, if desired by the contractors, who shall attend and survey the work and see that it be well executed, and at as moderate an expense as may be practicable: he shall likewise, examine and certify every account, so as to ascertain truly the actual amount necessarily expended.

7 To engage with such contractors as shall submit their operations to the controul of a superintendant.

First, That if the *tolls* fixed should, upon experience, be found so unproductive as not to yield, after paying annual charges, six per centum per annum, clear, upon the capital expended, the Board of Commissioners shall, in such case, pay the annual deficiency; or may annul such contract, on re-paying to the contractors the money expended.

Secondly, That on the contrary, where the *toll* shall be found so productive as to yield more than six per centum per annum, the Commissioners may, at the end of   years, annul such contract, paying back the capital sum with an advance of   per cent. to the proprietors. But if the contractors do do not agree to a public superintendant, or ask aid, it may be supposed that the contract is amongst the advantageous ones, and the Commissioners may, at the end of   years, annul the same, as above.

8. To authorize the contracting parties to establish fences and gates, at such distances as may be deemed necessary and proper, to enable the due collection of the tolls with the least possible inconvenience to travellers.

9. The several Boards of Contractors shall be declared, by law, to be corporations or bodies politic, for carrying into effect the purposes of their contracts, for and during the terms thereof; and shall be authorized,

First, To divide the capital sum expended into shares of   dollars each; and,

Secondly, To grant a certificate to every proprietor of a share, which shall be transferrable at pleasure, and every holder of a share, whilst he continues so to be, shall be a member of the corporation.

Thirdly, Each corporation shall have a right to elect a Treasurer and Managers, to conduct the affairs of the corporation, agreeably to such rules and regulations as it may, from time to time, establish.

Fourthly, Every share to entitle the holder to a vote in establishing *general rules* and *regulations*, and in the choice of the Treasurer and Managers.

Fifthly, The Managers to have power—

1st. To call upon the contractors, or subscribers, for such proportions, from time to time, of their respective subscriptions, as may be necessary to carry on the work until finished, placing the sums collected in the hands of the Treasurer.

2d. To employ workmen, purchase materials and conduct the whole business, either under their own inspection, or by their agent or agents.

3d. To settle all accounts, and draw orders upon the Treasurer for the payments, or advances, which ought to be made.

4th. To superintend the collection of the tolls, either by proper agents to be employed for the purpose, or by *farming* the same to individuals.

5th. To settle the accounts of the tolls, and make dividends half yearly, which shall be announced in the news-papers.

6th. To call the corporation together whenever they shall find necessary, and to lay their proceedings and accounts before it, at least once a year, and oftner if thereunto required by a quorum thereof.

9. The said Board of Commissioners to have the care and superintendency of *inland navigations*, respecting which they should be empowered,

First, To determine which of those that are proposed by the report of the committee of Assembly, shall be undertaken solely at the public expense, and which of them can be best performed by contractors entitled to tolls, &c. The latter to
be

be preferred whenever the situation, and nature of the improvements will admit of it. With respect to the former, the Board should be authorized to carry on the work at the public expense, under the direction of such agent or agents as they may appoint for that purpose. In regard to the latter, viz. such improvements as may be entitled to tolls, the Board should be empowered,

1st. To advertise for contracts.

2d. To appoint superintendants to examine, survey and report the works necessary to be performed.

3d. To make the contracts and engagements with individuals, or companies willing to undertake the same, and who are to be declared bodies politic, as proposed in the case of roads.

4th. The Commissioners shall also have power to fix the tolls, and to divide the capital into shares transferable, &c. as in the case of turnpike roads.

10. By an article in each contract, the government shall be restrained from laying out or establishing turnpikes, or toll navigations, in a second instance, that during   years, would destroy or diminish the income or revenue of turnpikes or toll navigations which they had established in the first instance.

11. The Board of Commissioners to be empowered to lend public money, if necessary, to any contractors or subscribers, to turnpike roads, or toll navigations, for the purpose of compleating what they have undertaken, if after going certain lengths, it should appear that they would be unable to compleat the same without such aid, sufficient security being given, that the sums so lent shall be faithfully applied to the uses intended, and re-paid at the end of the term stipulated. Or, the said Board may subscribe, on behalf of the commonwealth, such number of shares under any contract for turnpike roads or toll navigation, as may be found necessary, and be entitled to all the rights and privileges conferred on the share holders.

12. The Board of Commissioners shall make application to the Governor, for his warrant upon the Treasurer, for the sums of money which they may, from time to time, require for carrying their duty into effect; their requisitions to be made in writing, and to be founded upon estimates of expenditures necessary or actually made, or upon engagements, subscriptions, or contracts made for the purposes of their appointment, and the Governor to grant his warrants upon such requisition (to be paid out of the fund appropriated to this use) unless he shall see sufficient cause to refuse; in which case he shall assign his reasons in writing.

The Society have directed an accurate geographical and hydrographical *map* to be compiled from actual surveys; exhibiting a general and compleat view of the *roads* and *water* communications, which are proposed to be improved, connecting them with the roads and water communications of the neighbouring states; and they have promoted a liberal subscription for the immediate publication of the same; considering that such a map will not only be highly useful to all persons who wish to gain a general knowledge

F

ledge of the situation of the country, and the various improvements of which the state of Pennsylvania is susceptible, but it will likewise be useful to the public, by directing their attention to the different parts of the state which are the objects of improvement, and bringing forward individuals, as well as companies, to promote and undertake the execution of the same. But as the subscriptions of the members of the Society alone may not be sufficient encouragement for the publication of a map of such an expensive nature, the Society beg leave to recommend the further encouragement of the same to the Legislature, and herewith have presented the original draft of the same to their inspection. All which is humbly submitted.

By order and on behalf of the Society,

ROBERT MORRIS, *President.*

THE foregoing memorial, with the estimates and proposed plan of execution, having been referred by the Legislature to committees of their respective Houses, to confer with the committee of the Society of roads and navigation, and to report thereon; the result of the whole, after mature deliberation, was the adoption of the following general principles—

That the Legislature, although animated with the warmest zeal for the improvement of their country, by means of roads and inland navigation, yet could not subject the finances of the state (even if adequate) to the burden of the whole; yet they would make liberal appropriations of public money for the improvement of such roads and navigable waters, as lying too remote from the more populous parts of the country, and the inhabitants but thinly settled, rendered it impracticable for them either to improve their own roads and waters by subscriptions or the usual county taxes; and the profits of the tolls would yet be too small, to induce companies to undertake the work at their own expense; but that in the more settled parts of the country, especially near the metropolis, they would be ready to incorporate companies, for the gradual and progressive improvement of roads and waters, where the tolls would be sufficient to recompence the subscribers or stockholders, and the charge would fall according to justice upon those who were to be benefited, in proportion to the use they might make of such roads and waters.

The Legislature, therefore, in discharge of their part, and to set a laudable example of public spirit, made large appropriations by law, for the improvement of sundry roads and waters; [see the appendix.] They also passed the following acts of incorporation, viz.—

An act

(23)

An act to enable the Governor of this commonwealth to incorporate a company, for opening a canal and lock-navigation between the rivers Schuylkill and Susquehanna, by the waters of Tulpehoccon, Quittapahilla and Swatara, in the counties of Berks and Dauphin.

WHEREAS the opening a communication by water, for the transportation of the produce of the country, and of goods, wares and merchandizes, between the city of Philadelphia and the western and north-western counties of the state of Pennsylvania, will greatly tend to strengthen the bands of union between citizens inhabiting distant parts of a country governed by the same free and happy constitution and laws, to the encouragement of agriculture and manufactures, and the promotion of commerce: And whereas, from reports made by certain Commissioners appointed by the late Supreme Executive Council, in pursuance of an act of the General Assembly of this commonwealth in such case provided, it appears, that the waters of Tulpehoccon, Quittapahilla and Swatara, in the counties of Berks and Dauphin, united, by means of a canal and locks, will be sufficient for an inland navigation for the purposes aforesaid; and it is reasonable that the expense of procuring so great a convenience should be defrayed by the persons who will derive an immediate benefit by the use of it:

Section I. *Be it therefore enacted by the Senate and House of Representatives of the commonwealth of Pennsylvania, in General Assembly met, and it is hereby enacted by the authority of the same,* That Henry Drinker, Robert Hare, Joseph Hiester, George Latimer, George Fry, William Montgomery, and Samuel Miles, be, and they are hereby, appointed Commissioners, to do and perform the several duties herein after mentioned, that is to say; they shall and may, on or before the first day of December next, procure a book, and therein enter as follows: " We, whose names are " hereto subscribed, do promise to pay to the President, Managers and " Company of the Schuylkill and Susquehanna navigation, the sum of " four hundred dollars for every share of stock in the said company set " opposite to our respective names, in such manner and proportions, and " at such times, as shall be determined by the said President and Ma-" nagers, in pursuance of an act of the General Assembly of Pennsyl-" vania, entitled, " An act to enable the Governor of this common-" wealth to incorporate a company, for opening a canal and lock-navi-" gation between the rivers Schuylkill and Susquehanna, by the waters " of Tulpehoccon, Quittapahilla and Swatara, in the counties of Berks " and Dauphin;" and shall thereupon give notice in three of the public news-papers, printed in Philadelphia, one whereof shall be in the German language, for one calendar month at the least, of the time and place

Commissioners appointed;

their duties.

To open a subscription book, &c.

(24)

The subscription book to be kept open fifteen days, and how many shares may be subscribed; if a greater number, how to be distributed.

place when and where the said book will be opened to receive subscriptions of stock for the said company, at which time and place the said Commissioners, or any three of them, shall attend, and shall permit and suffer all persons who shall offer to subscribe in the said book, which shall be kept open for at least fifteen days, for any number of shares of the said stock, not exceeding ten by or for any one person or copartnership at one time, and, if need be, shall adjourn from time to time, as the said Commissioners shall find proper and necessary, until the number of subscriptions shall amount to one thousand shares of stock; and if, while the said subscription shall be open, a greater number of shares shall be applied for than will fill up the said number of shares, then the said Commissioners shall apportion the whole number of shares previously applied for, by lottery, to and among the persons who shall have subscribed, or offered to subscribe, before the said Commissioners shall have declared the subscription to be full, and the book closed; and when the said subscription shall be filled to the amount of five hundred shares, the said Commissioners shall return to the Governor of this commonwealth a full and perfect list of all the subscriptions to the said stock, with the number of shares by them respectively subscribed, certified under the hands and seals of the said Commissioners.

When 500 shares are subscribed, a return shall be made to the Governor.

Thereupon the Governor shall incorporate the subscribers.

Section II. *And be it further enacted by the authority aforesaid,* That whenever five hundred shares shall be subscribed to the capital stock of the company, that then it shall and may be lawful to and for the Governor of this commonwealth, by letters patent, under the great seal of the state, to create and erect the said subscribers into one body corporate and politic in deed, and in law, with perpetual succession, and with all the privileges and franchises incident to a corporation, by the name, stile and title of "The President, Managers and Company of the Schuylkill and Susquehanna navigation;" and by such name the said subscribers shall be able and capable, by force of this act and the said letters patent, of exercising all and singular the said privileges and franchises; and, moreover, shall be able and capable of holding their said capital stock, and the increase and profits thereof, and of enlarging the same, from time to time, by new subscriptions, in such manner and form as they shall think proper, if such enlargement shall be found necessary to fulfil the end and intent of this act; and of purchasing, taking and holding to them, their successors and assigns, in fee simple, or for any lesser estate, all such lands, tenements and hereditaments, as shall be necessary for them in the prosecution of their works; and of doing all and every other act, matter and thing, which a corporation or body politic may lawfully do.

The corporate stile,

and powers.

The first seven named patentees to give notice of a time

Section III. *And be it further enacted by the authority aforesaid,* That the first seven persons named in the said letters patent shall, as soon as conveniently may be after sealing the same, give notice in three of the newspapers,

(25)

papers, published in the city of Philadelphia as aforesaid, of a time and place by them to be appointed, not less than thirty days from the time of issuing the said notice, at which time and place the said subscribers shall proceed to organize the said corporation, and shall choose, by majority of votes of the said subscribers, by ballots, to be delivered in person or by proxy, one President, twelve Managers, one Treasurer, and such other officers as they shall think necessary to conduct the business of the said company, for one year, and until other such officers shall be elected; and shall or may make such bye-laws, rules, orders and regulations, not inconsistent with the constitution and laws of this commonwealth, as shall be necessary for the well ordering the affairs of the said company: *Provided always,* That no person shall have more than twenty votes in the said elections, or in determining any question arising at such meeting, whatever number of shares he may be entitled unto, and that each person holding one or more shares, under the said number of twenty, shall have one vote for every share by him held. *and place for choosing the officers of the corporation.*

No person to have more than twenty votes, but under that number there shall be a vote for each share.

Section IV. *And be it further enacted by the authority aforesaid,* That the said company shall meet on the first Monday of January, in each succeeding year, at such place within this state as shall be fixed by the rules and orders of the said company, to be made as aforesaid, for the purpose of choosing such officers as aforesaid for the ensuing year, and at such other time as they shall be assembled by the Managers for the purpose of making such further bye-laws, rules, orders and regulations, not inconsistent with the constitution and existing laws of this state, as shall from time to time, be necessary, of which meetings previous notice shall be given, in such manner as shall be provided by such rules and orders. *The time and place of meeting annually, for choosing officers, &c.*

Notice to be given of the meetings.

Section V. *And be it further enacted by the authority aforesaid,* That the said President and Managers shall procure certificates to be written or printed, for every share of the capital stock of the said company, and deliver one to each subscriber, signed by the President, and sealed with their common seal, he paying to the Treasurer of the company the sum of seventy-five dollars for every share by him subscribed, which certificate shall be transferable at his pleasure, in the presence of the Treasurer of the said company, subject, however, to all payments thereupon due and to grow due; and the holder of every such certificate, having first caused the assignment to him to be entered into a book of the company, to be kept for that purpose, shall be a member of the said corporation, entitled to one share of the capital stock, and of all the estate and emoluments of the company, and to vote as aforesaid at the general meetings thereof. *The subscribers to be furnished with certificates of their shares.*

The certificates transferable.

Section VI. *And be it further enacted by the authority aforesaid,* That the said President and Managers shall have full power and authority to appoint all officers necessary to supply vacancies by death, resignation, or otherwise, and also to appoint one or more superintendant of the works *Vacancies to be supplied;*

G to

and superintendants, &c. of the works appointed.	to be undertaken by them, and to hire and employ all such engineers, artists, workmen and labourers, as they shall find necessary to carry on the same; and by the said superintendant, engineers, artists, workmen and labourers, to enter into and upon all and singular the land and lands covered with the water situate upon, near, and between Tulpehoccon creek, in the county of Berks, and Swatara creek, in the county of Dauphin, and to lay out and survey such route or tracks as shall be most practicable for effecting a navigable canal between the rivers Schuylkill and Susquehanna, by means of locks and other devices, doing nevertheless as little damage as possible to the grounds and inclosures in and over which they shall pass; and thereupon it shall and may be lawful to and for the said President and Managers to contract and agree with the owners of any lands and tenements, for the purchase of so much thereof as shall be necessary for the purpose of making, digging and perfecting the said canal, and of erecting and establishing all the necessary locks, works and devices, to such a navigation belonging, if they can agree with such owners; but in case of disagreement, or in case the owner thereof shall be feme covert, under age, non compos mentis, or out of the state, then it shall and may be lawful to and for the said President and Managers to apply to two of the Justices of the Supreme Court of this commonwealth, who, upon such application, are hereby authorized and empowered, enjoined and required, to frame and issue one or more writ or writs, as occasion shall require, in the nature of a writ of ad quod damnum, to be directed to the Sheriff of the county in which such lands and tenements shall be, commanding him, that by the oaths and affirmations of twelve good and lawful men of his bailiwick, who shall be indifferent to the parties, he shall enquire whether the person or persons owning any lands and tenements necessary to be used by the said President and Managers, or which shall be injured in establishing the said canal and navigation, which person or persons shall be named, and which lands and tenements shall be described in such writ or writs, will suffer and sustain any, and what, damages, by reason or means of taking any lands, tenements, mill, mill-pond, water, water-course, or other real hereditament, necessary for the use of the said canal and navigation, and the locks and works thereto belonging, and to return the same writ, together with the finding of the said jury, to the next Supreme Court of this commonwealth after such finding; and upon such writ being delivered to the said Sheriff, he shall give at least ten days notice in writing to all and every the owners of the lands and tenements in the said writ described, of the time of executing the same, and shall cause to come upon the premises, at the time appointed, twelve good and lawful men of his bailiwick, who shall be selected in such manner as struck juries usually are, to whom he shall administer an oath or affirmation, that they will diligently enquire concerning the matters and things in the said writ specified, and a true verdict give according to the best of their skill and
The superintendants, &c. may enter upon all lands, &c. and lay out and survey the best track for a canal.	
The President &c. to agree with owners for the purchase of such lands, &c.	
In case of disagreement, or legal incapacity of the owners, a writ in the nature of a writ of ad quod damnum, shall issue from the Supreme Court.	
Proceedings on the writ.	
Return of the writ.	
Time of executing the writ to be notified to the owners of the lands, &c.	
A jury to be summoned and qualified;	

judgment,

judgment, without favor or partiality; and thereupon the said Sheriff and inquest shall proceed to view all and every the lands and tenements in such writ specified; and having considered the quantity of land, land covered with water, mills, buildings, or other improvements, that shall be necessary to be vested in the said company for the purposes aforesaid, and any water course then existing, the use whereof will be necessary for the purpose aforesaid, they shall cause the same to be minutely and exactly described by metes and bounds, or other particular descriptions, and shall value and appraise the injury or damages, if any, which the owner or owners of the said lands, tenements, mills, waters, water-courses, buildings, or improvements, will, according to their best skill and judgment, sustain and suffer, by means of so much of the said lands and tenements being vested in the said company, or by means of such improvements being destroyed, or rendered useless or of less value, or by means of the said company being permitted to turn such water to fill their canal and locks, or by means of said company being permitted to enlarge any mill-pond, mill-race, or other water-course, and to use the same as and for part of their said canal and navigation, or by any other means whatsoever, defining and ascertaining, as well all such lands and tenements, liberties and privileges, so to be vested in the said company, as the several sums at which the said injuries and damages shall be so assessed; and the said Sheriff and jury shall make an inquisition, under their hands and seals, distinctly and plainly setting forth all the matters and things aforesaid; and the Sheriff shall forthwith return the same, together with the said writ, to the office of the Prothonotary of the Supreme Court; and at the first Supreme Court which shall be held next after the return of any such writ, the Justices of the said court shall examine the same, and if the said writ shall appear to have been duly executed, and the return thereof be sufficiently certain to ascertain the lands and tenements, rights, liberties and privileges, intended to be vested in the said company, and the several compensations awarded to the owners thereof, then the said court shall enter judgment, that the said company, paying to the several owners as aforesaid the several sums of money in the said inquisition assessed, or bringing the same into the said court, over and besides the costs of such writ, and of executing and returning the same, shall be entitled to have and to hold to them, and their successors and assigns, for ever, all and every the lands, tenements, rights, liberties and privileges, in the said inquisition described, as fully and effectually as if the same had been granted to them by the respective owners thereof; and if any return so to be made shall not be sufficiently certain for the purposes aforesaid, the said court shall award an inquisition de novo.

they shall view the premises, and enquire of the damages;

and make an inquisition thereof under hand and seal, &c.

The Supreme Court to examine the writ and inquisition, and if duly issued and executed, shall give judgment that the company hold the premises, paying, &c.

Section VII. *And be it further enacted by the authority aforesaid*, That wherever the said canal shall cross any public or private laid out road or high-way, or shall divide the grounds of any person into two parts, so as

Proceedings, where the canal crosses a road.

as to require a ford or bridge to cross the same, the jury, who shall enquire of the damages to be sustained in manner herein directed, shall find and ascertain whether a passage across the same shall be admitted and maintained by a ford or by a bridge, and on such finding, the said President, Managers and Company shall cause a ford to be rendered practicable, or a bridge, fit for the passage of carts and waggons, to be built, and for ever hereafter maintained and kept in repair, at all and every the places so ascertained by the said jury, at the costs and charges of the said company; but nothing herein contained shall prevent any person from erecting and keeping in repair any foot or other bridge across the said canal, at his own expense, where the same shall pass through his ground, provided the same shall be of such height above the water as shall be usual in the bridges erected by the company; and provided also, that such foot or other bridges, so to be erected by the owners of such land, shall not interfere with any of the locks, buildings, or other works of the company.

Subscription money, how to be paid; and dividends, how to be received.

Section VIII. *And be it further enacted by the authority aforesaid,* That the said President and Managers shall have power and authority, from time to time, to fix the several sums of money which shall be paid by the subscriber or holder of every share of the stock of the said company, in part of the sum subscribed, and the time when each and every dividend, or part thereof shall be paid, and the place where it shall be received, and shall give at least thirty days notice in three of the public newspapers, published in the city of Philadelphia, as aforesaid, of the sum or dividend, and the time and place of receiving the same; and if any

Penalty on subscribers neglecting to pay.

holder of any share shall neglect to pay such proportions at the place aforesaid, for the space of sixty days after the time so appointed for paying the same, every such share holder, or his assignee, shall, in addition to the dividend so called for, pay after the rate of five per centum for every month's delay of such payment; and if the same, and the said additional penalty, shall not be paid for such space of time, as that the accumulated penalties shall become equal to the sums before paid for and on account of such shares, the same shall be forfeited to the said company, and may and shall be sold by them to any person or persons willing to purchase for such prices as can be obtained therefor.

The Corporation may enter upon lands, and carry away stone, gravel, &c. paying or tendering payment to the value.

Section IX. *And be it further enacted by the authority aforesaid,* That it shall and may be lawful to and for the said President and Managers, and their superintendants, engineers, artists, workmen and labourers, with carts, waggons, wains, and other carriages, with their beasts of draft and burthen, and all necessary tools and implements, to enter upon the lands contiguous or near to the said track of the intended canal and navigation, first giving notice of their intention to the owners thereof, and doing as little damage thereto as possible, and repairing any breaches they may make in the inclosures thereof, and making amends for any

damages

damages that may be sustained by the owners of such ground, by appraisement in manner hereinafter directed, and upon a reasonable agreement with the owners, if they can agree, or, if they cannot agree, then upon an appraisement to be made upon the oath or affirmation of three, or, if they disagree, any two indifferent freeholders, to be mutually chosen, or, if the owners neglect or refuse to join in the choice, to be appointed by any Justice of the Peace of the county, and tender of the appraised value, to carry away any stone, gravel, sand or earth, there being most conveniently situate for making or repairing the said canal and navigation, and to use the same in carrying on the said works.

Section X. *And be it further enacted by the authority aforesaid,* That it shall and may be lawful to and for the said President and Managers of the said company, so soon as the said canal and navigation, or any part thereof, shall be perfected, to appoint such and so many collectors of tolls for the passage of boats and vessels in, through, and along the same, and in such places as they shall think proper; and that it shall and may be lawful to and for such toll collectors, and their deputies, to demand and receive, of and from the persons having the charge of all boats and vessels, and rafts of timber, boards, plank, or scantling, passing through the said canal and navigation, and the locks thereto belonging, such tolls and rates for every ton weight of the ascertained burthen of the said boats and vessels, and for every hundred feet cubic measure of timber, and twelve hundred feet board measure of boards, plank or scantling, in rafts, as the said President and Managers shall think proper at any lock or other convenient place; provided that the amount of all the tolls, from the mouth of Swatara to the mouth of Tulpehoccon, shall not exceed in the whole the sum of one dollar for every ton of the burthen of such boat or vessel, and for every hundred feet cubic measure of timber, and twelve hundred feet board measure of boards, plank, or scantling, and so in proportion for any smaller distance and lesser number of locks, in any interval between the mouths of the said creeks.

Collectors of tolls to be appointed, when the canal, or any part is perfected.

Duty of the collectors and their deputies.

Limitation of the amount of tolls.

And in order to ascertain the tonnage of the boats using the said canal navigation, and to prevent disputes between the supercargoes and collectors of tolls concerning the same:

Section XI. *Be it further enacted by the authority aforesaid,* That upon the request of the owner, skipper, or supercargoe of such boat or raft, or of the collector of the said tolls at any lock upon the said canal and navigation, it shall and may be lawful for each of them to choose one skilful person to measure and ascertain the number of tons which the said boat or vessel is capable of carrying, and to mark the same in figures upon the head and stern of the said boat, in colours mixed with oil; and that the said boat or vessel, so measured and marked, shall always be permitted to pass through the said canal and locks for the price per ton, to which the number of tons so marked on her shall amount unto, agreeably to

Tonnage of boats using the canal, how to be ascertained, by agreement with the owner,

H
the

(30)

or in cafe the owner fhall decline the mode prefcribed. the rates fixed in the manner aforefaid; and if the owner, fkipper or fupercargoe of fuch boat or veffel fhall decline choofing a perfon, refident within four miles of the place where fuch toll is payable, to afcertain the tonnage thereof, then the amount of fuch tonnage fhall be fixed and afcertained by the perfon appointed for that purpofe by the faid Prefident and Managers, or chofen by the faid collector of tolls for the faid company, and the toll fhall be paid according to fuch meafurement, before any fuch boat or veffel fhall be permitted to pafs the lock or place where fuch toll fhall be made payable by the faid company.

Penalty for injuring the canal or works.
Section XII. *And be it further enacted by the authority aforefaid*, That if any perfon or perfons whatfoever fhall wilfully and knowingly do any act or thing whatfoever, whereby the faid navigation, or any lock, gate, engine, machine, or device, thereto belonging, fhall be injured or damaged, he or they fo offending fhall forfeit and pay to the faid company fourfold the cofts and damages by them fuftained, by means of fuch known and wilful act, together with cofts of fuit in that behalf expended, to be recovered by action of debt, in any court having jurifdiction competent to the fum due.

Collectors of tolls may ftop boats, or diftrain a part of the cargoe for tolls.

The diftrefs to be kept 5 days, and then fold.
Section XIII. *And be it further enacted by the authority aforefaid*, That the collectors of tolls, duly appointed and authorized by the faid Prefident and Managers, may ftop and detain all boats and veffels ufing the faid canal and navigation, until the owner, fkipper or fupercargoe of the fame fhall pay the tolls fo as aforefaid fixed, or may diftrain part of the cargoe therein contained, fufficient, by the appraifement of two credible perfons, to fatisfy the fame, which diftrefs fhall be kept by the collector of the tolls taking the fame for the fpace of five days, and afterwards be fold by public auction, at the moft public place in the neighbourhood, to the higheft bidder, in the fame manner and form as goods diftrained for rent are by law fold and faleable, rendering the furplus, if any there be, after payment of the faid tolls, and the cofts of diftrefs and fale, to the owner or owners thereof.

The perfons employed by the corporation to give bonds for performance of their refpective trufts.
Section XIV. *And be it further enacted by the authority aforefaid*, That the Prefident and Managers of the faid company may demand and require of and from the faid Treafurer, and of and from all and every other the fuperintendants, officers, and other perfons by them employed, bonds, in fufficient penalties, and with fuch fureties, as they fhall by their rules, orders and regulations, require, for the faithful difcharge of the feveral duties and trufts to them, or any or either of them, refpectively, committed.

The Prefident and Managers to keep accounts of all monies received and expended;
Section XV. *And be it further enacted by the authority aforefaid*, That the Prefident and Managers of the faid company fhall keep fair and juft accounts of all monies received by them from the fubfcribers to the faid undertaking, for their fubfcriptions thereto, and all penalties for delay
or

(31)

or non-payment thereof, and of all monies by them expended in the payment of the costs and charges of procuring and purchasing all estates, rights and titles, in the said company to be vested in pursuance of this act, or by any other means, and in paying their several officers by them to be appointed, and the wages of the different engineers, artists, workmen and labourers, by them to be employed, and for the materials and work furnished and done in the prosecution of the works projected by the said company, and shall, once at least in every year, submit such account to the general meeting of the stock holders, until the said canal and creeks therewith connected shall be rendered navigable, and until all the costs, charges and expenses of effecting the same shall be fully paid and discharged, and the aggregate amount of such expenses shall be liquidated; and from and after the liquidation thereof, if the one thousand shares above mentioned shall not be sufficient, it shall and may be lawful to and for the said President, Managers and Company, at a general meeting of the stock holders thereof, held in pursuance of the preceding provisions, or called by the President and Managers of the company for the especial purpose, by public notice in three news-papers in manner aforesaid (which shall be given three months previous to the opening of the said subscriptions) to increase the number of shares to such extent as shall be deemed sufficient to accomplish the object of this act, and to demand and receive such additional subscriptions from the former, or, in case of their neglect or refusal, from new subscribers, and upon such terms, and in such manner, as by the said general meeting shall be agreed upon; and the said President and Managers shall also keep a just and true account of all and every the monies received by their several and respective collectors of tolls in and through the said canal and navigation, from the one end thereof to the other, and shall make and declare a dividend of the clear profits and income thereof (all contingent costs and charges being first deducted) among all the subscribers to the said company's stock; and shall, on every the second Mondays of January and July, in every year, publish the half yearly dividend to be made of the said clear profits to and amongst the stock holders, and of the time and place when and where the same shall be paid; and shall cause the same to be paid accordingly.

they shall submit such account, at least once a year, to the stockholders, until the works are compleated, and the expenses discharged and liquidated. After such liquidation, the number of shares may be increased at a general meeting of the stockholders. Proceedings in such case.

The President, &c. to keep an account of tolls received;

and declare and pay a dividend of the profits half-yearly.

Section XVI. *And be it further enacted by the authority aforesaid,* That the said President and Managers shall, at the expiration of every third year from the date of their incorporation, lay before the General Assembly of this commonwealth an abstract of their accounts, shewing the whole amount of the capital expended in purchasing real estates, and in digging, erecting, and establishing the whole of the said canal, locks and works, and the whole income and profits arising from the said tolls for and during the said periods, together with the exact amount of the contingent charges of supporting, maintaining and keeping the same in repair for the said periods, to the end that the clear annual profits may

An abstract of the accounts to be laid before the General Assembly at the end of every third year.

Two years after the canal is completed, if the profits will not divide at the rate of six per cent. on the capital, the tolls may be encreased to make that amount.

A like abstract to be rendered every ten years, and if the profits will then divide at the rate of 25 per cent. on the capital, the tolls shall be reduced.

When the dividend shall amount to 15 per cent. on the capital, 1 per cent. shall be reserved for the establishment of schools, &c.

If the work is not carried on within two years, or is not finished within ten, the Legislature may resume the rights, &c. hereby granted.

be known; and if at the end of two years after the said canal and navigation shall be compleated, it shall appear that the said clear profits and income will not bear a dividend of six per centum per annum on the whole capital stock of the said company so expended, then it shall and may be lawful to and for the said President, Managers and Company, to increase the tolls herein above allowed to them, so much per ton through the whole length of the canal and navigation, and in proportion for each separate part thereof, as will raise the dividends up to six per centum per annum; and at the end of every period of ten years after the said canal shall be compleated, they shall render a like abstract to the General Assembly of their accounts for three preceding years, and if at the end of any such decennial period it shall appear, from such abstract, that the clear profits and income of the said company will bear a dividend of more than twenty five per centum per annum, then, and in such case, the said tolls shall be reduced so much per ton, as will reduce the said clear profits and income to a dividend not exceeding twenty-five per centum per annum.

Section XVII. *And be it further enacted by the authority aforesaid,* That whenever the profits of the said society shall amount to a clear annual dividend of fifteen per centum on the whole amount of their capital, there shall then be reserved one per centum out of the same, which shall be applied, at the direction of the Legislature, for the establishment of schools, and the encouragement of the arts and sciences, in one or more seminaries of learning, according to the provisions of the constitution.

Section XVIII. *And be it further enacted by the authority aforesaid,* That if the said company shall not proceed to carry on the said work within the space of two years from the passing of this act, or shall not, within the space of ten years from the passing of this act, compleat the same canal and navigation, so as to open an easy and safe water communication from the mouth of Swatara to the mouth of Tulpehoccon, navigable for boats of at least seven tons burthen, then, and in either of those cases, it shall and may be lawful for the Legislature of this commonwealth to resume all and singular the rights, liberties and privileges, hereby granted to the said company.

WILLIAM BINGHAM, *Speaker of the House of Representatives.*

RICHARD PETERS, *Speaker of the Senate.*

Approved, September the twenty-ninth, 1791.

THOMAS MIFFLIN, *Governor of the commonwealth of Pennsylvania.*

An act to enable the Governor of this commonwealth to incorporate a company, for opening a canal and water communication between the rivers Delaware and Schuylkill, and for other purposes therein mentioned.

WHEREAS connecting the waters of the rivers Delaware and Schuylkill, by means of a canal, will not only immediately contribute to the convenience of the citizens, but correspond with the extensive plan of connecting the eastern with the western waters of the state; and there being ample reasons for expecting that the same may be effected by individual citizens, if invited thereto by reasonable encouragement: Therefore,

Section I. *Be it enacted by the Senate and House of Representatives of the commonwealth of Pennsylvania, in General Assembly met, and it is hereby enacted by the authority of the same,* That David Rittenhouse, William Moore Smith, Elliston Perot, Cadwallader Evans, junior, and Francis Johnston, be, and they are hereby, appointed Commissioners, to do and perform the several duties hereafter mentioned; that is to say, they shall and may, on or before the first day of July next, procure a book or books, and therein enter as follows: " We, whose names are hereunto " subscribed, do promise to pay to the President and Managers of the " Delaware and Schuylkill canal navigation, the sum of two hundred " dollars, for every share of stock in the said company set opposite to our " respective names, in such manner and proportions, and at such times, " as shall be determined by the said President and Managers, in pur- " suance of an act of the General Assembly of this commonwealth, " entitled, " An act to enable the Governor of this commonwealth to " incorporate a company, for opening a canal and water communication " between the rivers Delaware and Schuylkill;" and shall thereupon give notice, in three of the public news-papers printed in Philadelphia, one whereof shall be in the German language, for one calendar month at the least, of the time and place, when and where the said book or books will be opened to receive subscriptions of stock for the said company; at which time and place the said Commissioners, or any three of them, shall attend, and shall permit and suffer all persons, who shall offer to subscribe in the said book or books, which shall, for that purpose, be kept open at least six hours in every juridical day, for the space of at least three successive days; and on any of the said juridical days, within the hours aforesaid, any person, of the age of twenty-one years, shall have liberty to subscribe in his own, or any other name or names, by whom he shall be authorized, for one share; on the second day, for one or two shares; on the third, for one, two or three shares; and on any succeeding day, while the said books shall remain open, for any number

Commissioners appointed to take subscriptions for establishing a canal between Schuylkill and Delaware.

Proceedings in taking subscriptions regulated.

of shares in the said stock; and if, at the expiration of the said three first days, the said book shall not have two thousand shares therein subscribed, the said Commissioners may adjourn, from time to time, until the said numbers of shares shall be subscribed, of which adjournments public notice shall be given in at least one public paper; and when the said subscriptions in the said books shall amount to the respective numbers aforesaid, the same shall respectively be closed; and if on that day, and before the said subscriptions shall be declared to be full, applications shall be made to subscribe more shares than will fill the said book to the numbers aforesaid, respectively, then the said Commissioners shall apportion the whole number of shares, unsubscribed on the morning of that day, among all those who shall have subscribed, or offered to subscribe, as aforesaid, on that day, by deducting from the subscribers of more shares than one, such proportion of the shares by them respectively subscribed, as will, with the least fraction, and leaving every person one or more shares, come nearest to the exact numbers of shares aforesaid: *Provided*

Deposit of ten dollars to be made on each share.

always, That every person offering to subscribe in the said book, in his own name, or any other name, shall previously pay to the attending Commissioners ten dollars for every share to be subscribed, out of which shall be defrayed the expenses attending the taking such subscriptions, and other incidental charges, and compensation to the said Commissioners, not exceeding two dollars to each of them for every day they shall be publicly employed in the said business, and the remainder shall be paid over to the Treasurer of the corporation, as soon as the same shall be organized, and the officers chosen, as herein after mentioned.

The commissioners to certify to the Governor when a certain number of shares are subscribed; and thereupon the subscribers shall be incorporated.

Stile and franchises of the corporation.

Section II. *And be it further enacted by the authority aforesaid*, That when one hundred persons, or more, shall have subscribed five hundred or more shares in the said stock, the said Commissioners may, or, when the whole number of shares aforesaid shall be subscribed, they shall certify, under their hands and seals, the names of the subscribers, and the number of shares subscribed by, or apportioned to, each subscriber, to the Governor of this commonwealth; and thereupon it shall and may be lawful to and for the Governor, by letters patent, under the great seal of the state, to create and erect such subscribers into one body, politic and corporate, in deed and in law, with perpetual succession, and with all the privileges and franchises incident to a corporation, by the name, stile and title, of " The President, Managers and Company of " the Delaware and Schuylkill canal navigation;" and by such name the said subscribers, and such other subscribers as may thereafter become shareholders, not exceeding the number of two thousand, as aforesaid, shall be able and capable of holding their said capital stock, and the increase and profits thereof, and of enlarging the same, from time to time, by new subscriptions, in such manner and form as they shall think proper, if such enlargement shall be found necessary to fulfil the end and intent of this act, and of purchasing, taking, and holding to them,

their

their successors and assigns, in fee simple, or for any lesser estate, all such lands, tenements and hereditaments, as shall be necessary for them in the prosecution of their work, and of doing all and every other act, matter and thing, which a corporation, or body politic, may lawfully do.

Section III. *And be it further enacted by the authority aforesaid,* That it shall and may be lawful for the said President and Managers to take water from the river Schuylkill by means of a canal, beginning at any place on the easterly side of the said river, between the upper side of the mouth of Stony creek, at Norriton, and the north bound of the city of Philadelphia, where it strikes the said river, and to conduct the water thereof, by means of a canal, along the easterly bank of the said river, or as near thereto as the nature of the ground and intervening obstacles and impediments will admit, and from thence to conduct the said water, as nearly parallel as may be, to the north bounds of the said city, by the most convenient route to the river Delaware, the width of the said canal, at or near the place where it shall be taken from the river Schuylkill, not to exceed thirty feet; and no more water shall be drawn from the said river, than will pass through a thirty feet water way, which shall be erected of stone or wood by the said company, and be kept in constant repair, under the penalty of forfeiting all the rights and immunities granted by this act; which water way shall be erected within the distance of one mile, at most, from the mouth of the said canal on the river Schuylkill; but no part of the said work shall be commenced, before the said President and Managers shall have ascertained and paid for the value of the ground to be occupied by the said canal and works, as also for any damage which the owners may sustain by means of such alienation, or otherwise, by means of the canal passing through their grounds, agreeably to the mode herein after directed: *Provided always,* That wherever the said President and Managers shall find it most convenient to commence the said canal, they shall have liberty to erect a wing from the easterly shore of the said river Schuylkill, extending up the stream, but not to extend more than one-third across the said river, except the said wing shall be erected at the upper side of the mouth of Stony creek, in which case it may extend to the head of the island opposite thereto, but the said canal shall not be commenced, and the said wing be erected, at any place which shall render the navigation of the said river dangerous, by forcing boats or rafts on the opposite shore, or on rocks or shoals, which they might otherwise have passed in safety; and if the said President and Managers shall be of opinion that it may be advisable to construct a canal between the said rivers Schuylkill and Delaware, by means of lock navigation, to be supplied with water from the streams lying between the north bounds of the city of Philadelphia and the distance of eight miles therefrom, it shall and may be lawful for them so to do, and, to effect the same, shall have power to conduct any of the said streams into such canal, paying for the damage occasioned thereby in manner aforesaid.

(margin notes:) Powers of the President and Managers to take water from the Schuylkill for the canal; course of the canal; its width; its construction. The owners of the ground to be first paid. President and Managers may erect a wing, extending up the stream. Restrictions with respect to such wing. Proceedings in case it is thought advisable to construct the canal by lock navigation, to be supplied from streams within eight miles of the north bound of Philadelphia.

(36)

Dry and wet docks may be formed near Philadelphia, and pipes to supply the neighbourhood with water.

Section IV. *And be it further enacted by the authority aforesaid,* That the said President and Managers shall have power to form dry and wet docks, for the accommodation of vessels, near the city of Philadelphia, to communicate with the waters of the said canal, and to supply the city of Philadelphia, and the neighborhood thereof, with water, by means of pipes and other conductors, under the public roads, streets and alleys, conveying water from thence for the use of such persons, as will agree to pay for the same such annual prices as shall be established by the said President and Managers: *Provided always,* That they shall immediately repair any injury which they may do to said roads, streets or alleys, by means of laying down or repairing any of the said pipes or conductors, and give as little obstruction to the use of the said roads, streets or alleys, as the nature of the works will admit: *Provided also,* That the said company shall not be entitled to any greater price for water to supply the city, and neighborhood thereof, than will create the annual profit of ten per centum on the capital that may and shall be expended for that particular purpose, exclusive of the general expense of the canal.

Injuries done to roads for such purpose to be immediately repaired.

For the supply of water for the city, ten per cent. is allowed.

Proceedings, to organize the corporation.

Section V. *And be it further enacted by the authority aforesaid,* That the seven persons first named in the said letters patent shall, as soon as conveniently may be after sealing the same, give notice in three of the newspapers, published in the city of Philadelphia as aforesaid, of a time and place by them to be appointed, not less than thirty days from the time of issuing the said notice, at which time and place the said subscribers shall proceed to organize the said corporation, and shall choose, by majority of votes of the said subscribers, by ballots, to be delivered in person or by proxy, one President, twelve Managers, one Treasurer, and such other officers as they shall think necessary to conduct the business of the said company, for one year, and until such other officers shall be elected; and shall or may make such bye-laws, rules, orders and regulations, not inconsistent with the constitution and laws of this commonwealth, as shall be necessary for the well ordering of the affairs of the said company: *Provided always,* That no person shall have more than twenty votes in the said elections, or in determining any question arising at such meeting, whatever number of shares he may be entitled to, and that each person holding one or more shares, under the said number of twenty, shall have one vote for every share by him held.

Times of meeting.

Section VI. *And be it further enacted by the authority aforesaid,* That the said company shall meet on the first Monday of January, in each succeeding year, at such place as shall be fixed by the rules and orders of the said company, to be made as aforesaid, for the purpose of choosing such officers as aforesaid for the ensuing year, and at such other times as they shall be assembled by the Managers for the purpose of making bye-laws, rules, orders and regulations, not inconsistent with the constitution and existing laws of this state, as shall from time to time, be necessary, of which meetings previous notice shall be given, in such manner as shall be provided by such rules and orders.

(37)

Section VII. *And be it further enacted by the authority aforesaid*, That the said President and Managers shall procure certificates to be printed or written, for every share of the capital stock of the said company, and deliver one to each subscriber, signed by the President, and sealed with their common seal, he paying to the Treasurer of the company the sum of twenty-five dollars for every share by him subscribed, which certificate shall be transferable at his pleasure, in the presence of the Treasurer of the said company, subject, however, to all payments due and to grow due; and the holder of every such certificate, having first caused the assignment to him to be entered into a book of the company, to be kept for that purpose, shall be a member of the said corporation, entitled to one share of the capital stock, and of all the estate and emoluments of the company, and to vote as aforesaid at the general meetings thereof. *Certificates of shares to be issued; which shall be transferable.*

Section VIII. *And be it further enacted by the authority aforesaid*, That the said President and Managers shall have full power and authority to appoint all officers necessary to supply vacancies by death, resignation, or otherwise, and also to appoint one or more superintendants of the works to be undertaken by them, and to hire and employ all such engineers, artists, workmen and labourers, as they shall find necessary to carry on the same; and by the said superintendant, engineers, artists, workmen and labourers, to enter into and upon all and singular the land and lands, which may be deemed most convenient for accommodating the said canal navigation, and to lay out and survey such route or tracks as shall be deemed most practicable for effecting a navigable canal between the rivers Delaware and Schuylkill, near the said city, by means of locks and other devices, conformably to the provisions in the third section of this act, doing, nevertheless, as little damage as possible to the ground and inclosures in and over which they shall pass; and thereupon it shall and may be lawful to and for the said President and Managers to contract and agree with the owners of any lands and tenements, for the purchase of so much thereof as shall be necessary for the purpose of making, digging and perfecting the said canal, and of erecting and establishing all the necessary locks, works and devices, to such a navigation belonging, if they can agree with such owners; but in case of disagreement, or in case the owner thereof shall be feme covert, under age, non compos mentis, or out of the state, or otherwise incapacitated to convey, then it shall and may be lawful to and for the said President and Managers to apply to two of the Justices of the Supreme Court of this commonwealth, who, upon such application, are hereby authorized and empowered, enjoined and required, to frame and issue one or more writ or writs, as occasion shall require, in the nature of a writ ad quod damnum, to be directed to the Sheriff of the county in which such lands and tenements shall be, commanding him, that by the oaths and affirmations *Vacancies to be supplied, and superintendants, &c. appointed, by the President and Managers. They may enter on lands &c. convenient for the canal; and contract with the owners for necessary parts thereof. Proceeding, in case of disagreement, or disqualification of the owner to convey.*

K

tions of twelve good and lawful men of his bailiwick, who shall be indifferent to the parties, he shall enquire whether the person or persons owning any lands and tenements necessary to be used by the said President and Managers, or which shall be injured in establishing the said canal and navigation, which person or persons shall be named, and which lands and tenements shall be described in such writ or writs, will suffer and sustain any, and what, damages, by reason or means of taking any such lands, tenements or other real hereditaments, necessary for the use of said canal and navigation, and the locks and works thereto belonging, and to return the same writ, together with the finding of the said jury, to the next Supreme Court of this commonwealth after such finding; and upon such writ being delivered to the said Sheriff, he shall give at least ten days notice in writing to all and every the owners, or their representatives, of the lands and tenements in the said writ described, of the time of executing the same, and shall cause to come upon the premises, at the time appointed, twelve good and lawful men of his bailiwick, who shall be selected in such manner as struck juries usually are, to whom he shall administer an oath or affirmation, that they will diligently enquire concerning the matters and things in the said writ specified, and a true verdict give according to the best of their skill and judgment, without favor or partiality; and thereupon the said Sheriff and inquest shall proceed to view all and every the lands and tenements, or other real hereditaments, in such writ specified, and having considered the quantity and quality thereof, which shall be necessary to be vested in the said company, for the purposes aforesaid, they shall cause the same to be minutely and exactly described, by metes and bounds, or other particular descriptions, and shall value and appraise the injury and damages which the owner or owners of the said lands, tenements, or other real hereditaments or improvements, will, according to their best skill and judgment, sustain and suffer, by means of so much of the said lands, tenements, or other real hereditaments or improvements, being vested in the said company, or by means of any works being destroyed, or rendered useless or of less value, or by means of the said company being permitted to turn any water course, for the use of the said canal, or by means of said company being permitted to enlarge any pond or water course, and to use the same for the purposes aforesaid, or by any other means whatsoever, defining and ascertaining, as well all such lands and tenements, liberties and privileges, so to be vested in the said company, as the several sums at which the said injuries and damages shall be so assessed; and the said Sheriff and jury shall make an inquisition, under their hands and seals, distinctly and plainly setting forth all the matters and things aforesaid, and the Sheriff shall forthwith return the same, together with the said writ, to the office of the Prothonotary of the Supreme Court; and at the first Supreme Court which shall be held next after the return of any such writ, the Justices of the said court shall examine the same, and if the said writ shall appear to have been duly executed, and the return thereof be sufficient to ascertain the lands and tenements, rights, liberties and privileges, intended to be vested in the said company, and the several compensations awarded to the owners thereof, then the said court shall enter judgment, that the said company, paying to the several owners, as aforesaid, the several sums of money in the said inquisition assessed, or bringing the same into the said court, over and besides the cost of such writ, and of executing and returning the same, shall be entitled to have and to hold to them, and their successors and assigns for ever, all and every the lands, tenements, rights, liberties and privileges, in the said inquisition described, as fully and effectually, as if the same had been granted to them by the respective owners thereof; and if any return so to be made shall not be sufficiently certain for the purposes aforesaid, the said court shall award inquisition de novo.

Section IX. *And be it further enacted by the authority aforesaid*, That whenever the said canal shall cross any public or private laid out road or highway, or shall divide the grounds of any person into two parts, so as to require a ford or bridge to cross the same, the jury, who shall enquire of the damages to be sustained in manner herein directed, shall find and ascertain whether a passage across the same shall be admitted and maintained by a ford or bridge, and on such finding, the said President, and Managers and Company shall cause a ford to be rendered practicable, or a bridge, fit for the passage of carts and waggons, to be built, and for ever after maintained and kept in repair, at all and every the places so ascertained by the said jury, at the costs and charges of the said company; but nothing herein contained shall prevent any person from erecting and keeping in repair any foot or other bridge across the said canal, at his own expence, where the same shall pass through his ground, provided the same shall be of such a height above the water as shall be usual in the bridges erected by the company; and provided that such foot or other bridges, so to be erected by the owners of such lands, shall not interfere with any of the locks, or buildings, or other works of the company. *In what cases bridges shall be erected across the canal.*

Section X. *And be it further enacted by the authority aforesaid*, That the said President and Managers shall have power and authority, from time to time, to fix the several sums of money which shall be paid by the subscriber or holder of every share of the stock of the said company, in part, or for the sum subscribed, and the time when each and every dividend or part thereof shall be paid, and the place where it shall be received, and shall give at least thirty days notice in three of the public newspapers, published in the city of Philadelphia, as aforesaid, of the sum or dividend, and the time and place of receiving the same; and if the holder of any share shall neglect to pay such proportions at the place aforesaid, for the space of sixty days after the time so appointed for paying *Subscription, how and when to be paid.*

Penalty on neglect to pay.

(40)

ing the same, every such share holder, or his assignee, shall, in addition to the dividend so called for, pay after the rate of five per centum for every month's delay of such payment; and if the same, and the said additional penalty, shall not be paid for such space of time, as that the accumulated penalties shall become equal to the sums before paid for and on account of such shares, the same shall be forfeited to the said company, and may and shall be sold by them to any person or persons willing to purchase for such prices as can be obtained therefor.

Mode of obtaining materials for the work from contiguous lands.

Section XI. *And be it further enacted by the authority aforesaid*, That it shall and may be lawful to and for the said President and Managers, and their superintendants, engineers, artists, workmen and labourers, with carts, waggons, wains, and other carriages, with their beasts of draft and burthen, and all necessary tools and implements, to enter upon the lands contiguous or near to the said track of the intended canal and navigation, first giving notice of their intention to the owners thereof, or their representatives, and doing as little damage thereto as possible, and repairing any breaches they may make in the inclosures thereof, and making amends for any damages that may be sustained by the owners of such ground, by appraisement in manner hereinafter directed, and upon a reasonable agreement with the owners, if they can agree, or, if they cannot agree, then upon an appraisement to be made upon the oath or affirmation of three, or, if they disagree, any two indifferent freeholders, to be mutually chosen, or, if the owners neglect or refuse to join in the choice, to be appointed by any Justice of the Peace of the county, and tender of the appraised value, to carry away any stone, gravel, sand or earth, thereon, being most conveniently situate for making or repairing the said canal and navigation, and to use the same in carrying on the said works.

Collectors of the tolls, how and where to be established.

Section XII. *And be it further enacted by the authority aforesaid*, That it shall and may be lawful to and for the said President and Managers of the said company, so soon as the said canal and navigation shall be perfected, to appoint such and so many collectors of tolls for the passage of boats, vessels and rafts, in and through and along the same, and in such places as they shall think proper; and that it shall and may be lawful to and for such toll collectors, and their deputies, to demand and receive, of and from the persons having the charge of all boats, vessels and rafts, passing through the said canal and navigation, and the locks thereto belonging,

What tolls shall be paid;

such tolls and rates, for every ton weight of the ascertained burthen of the said boats and vessels, and for every hundred feet, cubic measure, of timber, and twelve hundred feet, board measure, of boards, plank or scantling, in rafts, as the said President and Managers shall think proper,

and limitation of the amount.

at any lock or other convenient place at the said canal; provided that the amount of the said tolls shall not, in the whole, exceed the rate of one-sixteenth of a dollar per mile, for every ton of the burthen of such boat or vessel, and for every hundred feet, cubic measure, of timber, and twelve hundred feet, board measure, of boards, plank or scantling.

Section XIII. *And be it further enacted by the authority aforesaid,* That in order to ascertain the size of rafts and the tonnage of boats using and passing the said canal and navigation, and to prevent disputes between the supercargoes and collectors of tolls concerning the same, upon the request of the owner, skipper, or supercargoe of such boat or raft, or of the collector of the said tolls, at any lock upon the said canal and navigation, it shall and may be lawful for each of them to choose one skilful person to measure and ascertain the size of the said rafts, or the number of tons which the said boat or vessel is capable of carrying, and to mark the said tonnage, so ascertained, in figures, upon the head and stern of the said boat, in colours mixed with oil, and that the said boat or vessel, so measured and marked, shall be permitted to pass through the said canal and locks, for the price per ton to which the number of tons so marked on her shall amount to, agreeably to the rates fixed in the manner aforesaid; and if the owner, skipper or supercargoe of such boat or vessel shall decline choosing a person resident within two miles of the place where such toll is payable, to ascertain the tonnage thereof, then the amount of such tonnage shall be fixed and ascertained by the person appointed for that purpose by the President and Managers, or chosen by the said collector of tolls for the said company, and the toll shall be paid according to such measurement, before any such boat or vessel shall be permitted to pass the place where such toll shall be made payable by the said company. *Provided always,* That if any of the said boats shall have been marked on any other canal, the said collectors may admit the same as the rate of tonnage, unless they shall have cause to suspect that the same is not correct, in which case a new mark be painted, without defacing the old mark.

Mode of ascertaining the size of rafts and the tonnage of boats.

Section XIV. *And be it further enacted by the authority aforesaid,* That if any person or persons whatsoever shall wilfully and knowingly do any act or thing whatsoever, whereby the said navigation, or any lock, gate, engine, machine, or device, thereto belonging, shall be injured or damaged, he or they so offending shall forfeit and pay to the said company fourfold the costs and damages by them sustained, by means of such known and wilful act, together with costs of suit in that behalf expended, to be recovered by action of debt, in any court having jurisdiction competent to the sum due.

Penalty on injuring the works.

Section XV. *And be it further enacted by the authority aforesaid,* That the collectors of tolls, duly appointed and authorized by the said President and Managers, may stop and detain all boats and vessels using the said canal and navigation, and also all rafts passing the same, until the owner, skipper or supercargoe of the same, shall pay the tolls so as aforesaid fixed, or may distrain part of the cargoe therein contained, or a part of such rafts, sufficient, by the appraisement of two credible persons, to satisfy the toll, which distress shall be kept by the collector of the tolls

Payment of tolls, how to be enforced.

(42)

tolls taking the same for the space of five days, and afterwards sold by public auction, at some public place in the neighbourhood, to the highest bidder, in the same manner and form as goods distrained for rent are by law sold and saleable, rendering the surplus, if any there be, after payment of the said tolls, and the costs of distress and sale, to the skipper, supercargoe or owners thereof.

The officers of the company to give security.

Section XVI. *And be it further enacted by the authority aforesaid,* That the President and Managers of the said company may demand and require of and from the said Treasurer, and of and from all and every other the officers, superintendants, and other persons by them employed, bonds, in sufficient penalties, and with such sureties, as they shall by their rules, orders and regulations require, for the faithful discharge of the several duties and trusts to them, or any of them, respectively, committed.

The President and Managers to keep accounts of the receipts and expenditures, till the whole is compleated.

The capital stock, how it may be increased.

Section XVII. *And be it further enacted by the authority aforesaid,* That the President and Managers of the said company shall keep fair and just accounts of all monies received by them, from the subscribers to the said undertaking, for their subscriptions thereto, and all penalties for delay or non-payment thereof, and of all monies by them expended in the payment of the costs and charges of procuring and purchasing all estates, rights and titles, in the said company to be vested in pursuance of this act, or by any other means, and in paying their several officers by them to be appointed, and the wages of the different engineers, artists, workmen and labourers, by them to be employed, and for the materials and work furnished and done in the prosecution of the works projected by the said company, and shall, once at least in every year, submit such account to the general meeting of the stock holders, until the said canal and navigation shall be compleated, and until all the costs, charges and expenses of effecting the same shall be fully paid and discharged, and the aggregate amount of such expenses shall be liquidated; and from and after the liquidation thereof, if the works shall not be sufficiently perfected, or from any casualty should be injured, so as to require an increase of the capital stock, it shall and may be lawful to and for the said President, Managers and Company, at a general meeting of the stock holders thereof, held in pursuance of the preceding provisions, or called by the President and Managers of the company for the especial purpose, by public notice in three news-papers in manner aforesaid (which shall be given three months previously to the opening of the said subscriptions) to increase the number of shares to such extent as shall be deemed sufficient to accomplish the object of this act, and to demand and receive such additional subscriptions from the former, or, in case of their neglect or refusal, after ten successive days from the time of such meeting, from new subscribers, and upon such terms, and in such manner, as by the said general meeting shall be agreed on.

Section

Section XVIII. *And be it further enacted by the authority aforesaid,* That the said President and Managers shall also keep a just and true account of all and every the monies received by their several and respective collectors of tolls on the said canal navigation, and shall make and declare a dividend of the clear profits and income thereof (all contingent costs and charges being first deducted) among all the subscribers to the said company's stock, and shall, on every the second Mondays of January and July, in every year, publish the half yearly dividend to be made of the said clear profits to and amongst the stock holders, and of the time and place, when and where the same shall be paid, and shall cause the same to be paid accordingly. The President and Managers to keep account of tolls received by collectors, and make the dividends.

Section XIX. *And be it further enacted by the authority aforesaid,* That the said President and Managers shall, at the expiration of every third year from the date of their incorporation, lay before the General Assembly of this commonwealth an abstract of their accounts, shewing the whole amount of the capital expended in purchasing real estates, and in digging, erecting, and establishing the whole of the said canal, locks and works, and the whole income and profits arising from the same, for and during the said periods, together with the exact amount of the contingent expenses of supporting, maintaining and keeping the same in repair for the said periods, to the end that the clear annual profits may be known; and if, at the end of two years after the said canal and navigation shall be compleated, it shall appear that the said clear profits and income will not bear a dividend of six per centum per annum on the whole capital stock of the said company so expended, then it shall and may be lawful to and for the said President, Managers and Company, to increase the tolls herein above allowed to them so much per ton, as will raise the dividend up to six per centum per annum; and at the end of every period of ten years after the said canal shall be compleated, they shall render a like abstract to the General Assembly of their accounts for three preceding years; and if, at the end of any such decennial period, it shall appear, from such abstract, that the clear profits and income of the said company will bear a dividend of more than twenty five per centum per annum, then, and in such case the said tolls shall be reduced so much per ton, as will reduce the said clear profits and income to a dividend not exceeding twenty-five per centum per annum. President and Managers to lay their accounts before the Legislature.

Proceedings, in case the profits will not divide six per cent.

or exceed twenty-five per cent.

Section XX. *And be it further enacted by the authority aforesaid,* That whenever the profits of the said company shall amount to a clear annual dividend of fifteen per centum on the whole amount of their capital stock expended, there shall then be reserved one per centum per annum out of the same, which shall be applied, under the direction of the Legislature for the establishment of schools, and the encouragement of the arts and sciences, in one or more seminaries of learning. When the profits divide fifteen per cent. one per cent. to be reserved for the public.

Section

(44)

Limitation for commencing and compleating the work.

Section XXI. *And be it further enacted by the authority aforesaid,* That if the said company shall not proceed to carry on the said work within the space of two years from the passing of this act, or shall not, within the space of ten years from the passing of this act, compleat the same canal and navigation, so as to open an easy and safe water communication from the river Schuylkill to the river Delaware, which canal or water shall be of the depth of three feet, and the width of at least twenty-four feet, then, and in either of those cases, it shall and may be lawful for the Legislature of this commonwealth to resume all and singular the rights, liberties and privileges, hereby granted to the said company.

WILLIAM BINGHAM, *Speaker of the House of Representatives.*

SAMUEL POWEL, *Speaker of the Senate.*

Approved, April the tenth, 1792.

THOMAS MIFFLIN, *Governor of the commonwealth of Pennsylvania.*

An act to incorporate the Conewago Canal Company.

WHEREAS the General Assembly of this commonwealth did, in and by an act, entitled " An act to provide for the opening and improving sundry navigable waters and roads within this commonwealth," authorize and empower the Governor to contract with individuals or companies, among other things, for improving the navigation of the river Susquehanna, from Wright's ferry to the mouth of Swatara creek, inclusive, and for that purpose appropriated the sum of five thousand two hundred and fifty pounds: And whereas a contract and articles of agreement were made and entered into on the third day of July, in the year of our Lord one thousand seven hundred and ninety-two, between Thomas Mifflin, Governor of the commonwealth of Pennsylvania, on behalf of the state, of the one part, and Robert Morris, William Smith, Walter Stewart, Samuel Meredith, John Steinmetz, Tench Francis, John Nicholson, John Donaldson, Samuel Miles, Timothy Matlack, David Rittenhouse, Samuel Powel, Alexander James Dallas, William Bingham, Henry Miller, Abraham Witmer and Robert Harris, all of the state of Pennsylvania, of the other part, as a company, by the name of The Conewago company, for opening and improving that part

part of the river Sufquehanna, from Wright's ferry to the mouth of Swatara creek, inclufive, agreeably to the true intent, meaning and defign of the Legiflature, whereby the faid Robert Morris and others, as a company, and each of them, did agree, undertake, and contract, to and with the faid Thomas Mifflin, and his fucceffors, Governors of the faid commonwealth, that they, the faid company, will well and truly open and improve the navigation of the faid river Sufquehanna, between Wright's ferry and the mouth of Swatara aforefaid, agreeably to the true intention of the Legiflature, in the manner fet forth in the faid contract, reference being thereto had at large: and, particularly, that at the Conewago falls they will one, eftablish and maintain a canal, of a fufficient and convenient width not lefs than forty feet, of a length fufficient to pafs and extend beyond all obftructions created in the navigation of the faid river by means of the faid Conewago falls, and of a depth fufficient at all times to contain and convey, through the whole diftance of the faid canal, a body of water, at leaft four feet deep; and that they will alfo erect and maintain on the faid canal a fufficient number of fafe and commodious locks, not lefs than two, for the benefit of navigation; and that the faid canal and locks, and the works thereunto belonging, fhall be for ever kept and maintained in good and perfect order and repair, by them, the faid contractors, their heirs, executors, adminiftrators, and affigns, at the proper coft of them, and every of them, and opened as a public highway and for public ufe for ever, fo that all perfons whofoever, with boats, rafts, and other fuitable veffels, and their freights, may thenceforth, at all feafons when the navigation of the faid river Sufquehanna is not rendered impracticable by ice, pafs and repafs in the faid canal, and ufe and enjoy the benefit of the faid locks, free of toll, and any and every other charge whatfoever, as freely as if the faid canal and locks, were made and eftablifhed by the public, and duly declared by law to be a public highway: And whereas the faid Thomas Mifflin, in behalf of this commonwealth, in confideration of the undertakings and contracts of the faid company, did covenant and agree, that they fhall have and receive the fum of five thoufand two hundred and fifty pounds, the fum appropriated by law, to be taken as full fatisfaction and compenfation of all their fervices and expenfes in carrying on, compleating, and maintaining the faid works: And whereas it has been reprefented to the Legiflature by the faid company, that no provifion having been made by the public to purchafe the ground through which the faid canal is to pafs, for the diftance of three hundred and fix perches, more or lefs, nor to compel the owners to part with the fame, at a reafonable price or valuation, for the public ufe, and that they have been obliged to purchafe the fame at their own expenfe, and at a very high rate, appropriating to the ufe of the public fuch part of their grounds as may be neceffary to the faid canal and works, the whole of which is to be conftructed and maintained within the grounds fo purchafed; but

M that

(45)

that in the execution of the said important work, for the public use and benefit, as well as for securing and maintaining the necessary constructions and erections from trespasses and damages, the better managing their several shares, dividing and transferring the same, making and executing contracts for carrying on the work, and the improvement of the natural advantages of their estates and interest in the lands contiguous to and connected with the said canal (including the ferry at the lower end of the said Conewago falls) they labor under many inconveniences, as a number of individuals bound by temporary articles to the execution and support of a public work, for permanent and perpetual use to the community at large, and have therefore prayed, that they may be constituted into a body politic and corporate, with the powers, rights and privileges, incident and necessary to a corporation of the like nature and kind:

The contractors for improving the navigation of the Susquehanna, at Conewago falls, incorporated.

Section I. *Be it therefore enacted by the Senate and House of Representatives of the commonwealth of Pennsylvania, in General Assembly met, and it is hereby enacted by the authority of the same*, That the said Robert Morris, William Smith, Walter Stewart, Samuel Meredith, John Steinmetz, Tench Francis, John Nicholson, John Donaldson, Samuel Miles, Timothy Matlack, David Rittenhouse, Samuel Powel, Alexander James Dallas, William Bingham, Henry Miller, Abraham Witmer, and Robert Harris, their successors and assigns, shall be, and they are hereby, incorporated into a body politic and corporate, in deed and in name, by the name, stile and title of "The Conewago Canal Company;" and by the same name, stile and title, they shall have succession for ever, and be able and capable in law to sue and be sued, to implead and be impleaded, and to have and to make one common seal, to use in their affairs, and the same to break and alter at their pleasure; and to hold and enjoy any lands, terements, goods, wares and merchandize, and all manner of estates, real and personal, and mixed, provided the same shall not exceed, at any time, one million of dollars; and shall have power to meet, choose, appoint and contract with all officers, servants, and persons necessary in the management of their affairs, and to do and perform such acts, and to make such rules, ordinances, bye-laws and regulations, (not inconsistent with the laws of the United States and of this state) as they, or a majority of them, shall from time to time find convenient, useful, and necessary for establishing and maintaining the said canal and locks, and the works thereunto belonging, or connected with the same; and in general for the better managing and promoting the interests of the said corporation and company, and the improvement of the natural advantages of their estate in the premises, in as full and ample a manner as any other corporate body within this commonwealth can or may do.

Section II. *And be it further enacted by the authority aforesaid*, That the said canal and locks shall be, and the same are hereby declared to be, a public highway, and as such shall be kept and maintained by the said corporation

corporation and company, for public use, for ever, so that all persons with boats, rafts, and other suitable vessels, with their freights, may at all seasons, when the navigation of the river Susquehanna and the said canal is not rendered impracticable by ice, pass and re-pass in the same, and use and enjoy the benefit of the said locks, free of toll, and any and every other charge whatsoever; and the said company shall keep and maintain a skilful person for opening and shutting the locks, for assisting the boatmen in their passage through the same.

The canal and locks to be established at the Conewago falls declared a public highway, and to be kept as such by the company.

Section III. *And be it further enacted by the authority aforesaid,* That if any person or persons whatsoever shall, wilfully and knowingly, do any act or thing whatsoever, whereby the said navigation, or any lock, gate, engine, machine or device, thereto belonging, shall be injured or damaged, he, she or they, so offending, shall forfeit and pay to the said company fourfold the costs and damages by them sustained by means of such known and wilful act, together with costs of suit in that behalf expended, to be recovered, by action of debt, before any Justice of the Peace, or in any court having jurisdiction competent to the sum due.

Penalty for injuring the canal or its works.

Section IV. *Provided always, and be it further enacted by the authority aforesaid,* That nothing in this act contained shall be held, deemed, taken, or in any wise understood, to invalidate the contract had and made between the Governor of this commonwealth and the said company, for compleating the said canal and locks in the manner, and in the time, therein specified, nor to release the said company, or any of them, from their responsibility, each for the other, jointly and severally, in the due and faithful execution of the work, according to the true intention of the Legislature, as specified and set forth in the said contract.

This act not to invalidate the contract formed with the Governor.

      GERARDUS WYNKOOP, *Speaker*
        of the House of Representatives.

       SAMUEL POWEL, *Speaker*
          of the Senate.

Approved, April the tenth, 1793.

     THOMAS MIFFLIN, *Governor*
      of the commonwealth of Pennsylvania.

                Schuylkill

Schuylkill and Susquehanna Canal Navigation.

To the Senate and House of Representatives of the commonwealth of Pennsylvania, in General Assembly met:—

THE President, Managers and Company of the Schuylkill and Susquehanna navigation, with every sentiment of respect and grateful acknowledgment of that protection, encouragement and support, which they have received from the Legislature in the carrying on the great work committed to their trust and direction; beg leave to submit, to the consideration of the General Assembly, an account of the work already executed, the monies expended, the plan and probable expense of the work remaining to be accomplished, and the prospect of an effectual completion of the whole undertaking, within the time limited by law.

The magnitude and immense importance of the system of *roads and inland navigation*, projected, and now in rapid progress, through the various parts of the state, as tending to the increase of our *commercial* and *agricultural* interest, to the general prosperity of our citizens of every class and degree, and strengthening the bands of their union to the most distant parts of the state, need not be mentioned to an enlightened Legislature; which hath nursed this *great work*, by the aid of public money from the beginning, and hath incorporated and encouraged companies with liberal franchises, for carrying on and completing the same.

Within the whole habitable globe, there is not a country, of equal dimensions, which offers to its industrious inhabitants more resources of wealth, independence and happiness, than Pennsylvania; considering the salubrity of climate, the fertility of soil, the variety of produce and manufacturing materials, and the means of communication by *improved roads* and the *inland navigation* of our great rivers and their numerous branches, embracing and interlocking with each other, and spreading themselves (up to their sources) through all the parts of the state; and forming *water communications* by sundry routs, from the *tide waters* of *Delaware* and the *Atlantic*, to the great lakes and extreme bounds of the United States.

The CANAL which is to connect the *Schuylkill* and *Susquehanna* navigation is the *chief link* of this vast chain—a link on which the success and utility of the whole must necessarily depend.

The summit level of this *canal*, between Lebanon and Myers-town, for upwards of three miles is compleated, in respect to the heavy digging, and the purchase of all the ground for the scite of the canal, the locks and towing paths; as well as the grounds containing the sources and springs of the waters, and through which they are to be conducted into the *reservoir* at the summit level. The exhorbitant prices allowed by *juries* for some of the lands and waters necessary to the work, has considerably enhanced the expense of this part; but a sufficiency of water to fill the *canal* and *locks* at the middle

dle ground, was of such essential consequence to the success of the undertaking, that the whole system of our inland navigation must have been deranged, and have become abortive, if the Managers had been deterred, or slackened their exertions, on account of the expense; which, after all, does not greatly or disproportionably exceed the original estimates for the middle ground; and the final amount of expenditures on this part will not be above *forty thousand pounds.*

The two remaining parts of this grand communication under our direction, are—

1. The *Tulpehocken canal navigation,* from the east end of the middle ground, down to Schuylkill at the mouth of Tulpehocken; being, by the courses of the creek and along its margin, thirty-five miles.

2. The *Quitipahilla* and *Swatara* navigation, from Lebanon to Susquehanna, being thirty-two miles.

The report of our engineer, his plan and estimates, together with his able and judicious arguments and reasons for preferring, generally, a CANAL NAVIGATION along the margin, to the natural bed of the waters, (as being a more compleat navigation, with less injury to the meadows or mills of the land holders, and on the whole, at an expense not so much greater as to be placed in competition with the permanent advantages to be derived from it) are herewith submitted to the Legislature.

But the original calculations, on framing the act by which we were incorporated, were grounded upon the presumption that the natural beds of those rivers, by means of *dams* and *locks,* might answer the purpose of a temporary navigation, with little more than eight or ten miles digging on the whole; whereas, on the present improved plan, (which will remain of permanent emolument to the state, so long as those rivers continue to run) the expense will be about thrice the sum first contemplated, as will appear by the annexed estimate—It is an expense however, (considering the magnitude of the undertaking) which can by no means be viewed as beyond the powers of this state, and is a prize worthy of their public spirit, and utmost exertions to be accomplished.—Your memorialists therefore, cannot but entertain the most sanguine expectations of the aid and encouragement of the Legislature in prosecuting and compleating the work.

By the estimates hereto annexed, it will appear, that in order to compleat the navigation upon a permanent foundation, through the distance of about seventy miles (from the mouth of Tulpehocken on Schuylkill, to the mouth of Swatara, on Susquehanna) there will be a deficiency of £. 308,000—but the trade which may reasonably be expected through this immense communication with the Western World, will amply compensate the *public,* as well as the individual stockholders, for the *capital stock* to be employed in the work.

There are but two ways to raise this CAPITAL—

1. Either by enlarging the present *capital* by the increase of shares and new subscriptions, on the terms of the act of incorporation; or,

2. By the company's negociating and obtaining an *effectual loan.*

A *loan*, in the opinion of the stockholders and agreeably to their resolutions, at a meeting held to consider of the state of their affairs, is the mode they would prefer; and therefore they have instructed the President and Managers to pray the Legislature, and they accordingly pray—

For an aid in money to the amount of the said deficiency, or as much thereof as the Legislature may think proper to grant, either by lending the same to the company on interest, at the rate of six per centum per annum (the principal of the loan to be advanced, by the state, to the company, in monthly instalments of ten thousand dollars each;) or by the state taking an interest in the work, for the speedy accomplishment of the same, to the amount of the deficient capital, or such part thereof, as, in regard to the public emolument, they may think meet; and that, in case the loan shall be granted as aforesaid, the corporation engage to pay the same with interest, by instalments of not less than *fifty thousand dollars* annually; the first instalment to be paid at the end of twelve months after the work shall be finished, and the commencement of tolls thereon.

That, as by the act of incorporation, although some parts of the said *canal navigation* may be finished and in use, before the whole distance of *seventy* miles can be compleated; yet the Company are not enabled to receive toll for that part, except at the rate of one dollar for seventy miles, or the whole distance, which is only one cent and three-sevenths of a cent per mile; whereas the Delaware and Schuylkill canal is allowed one-sixteenth of a dollar per mile, whenever any part thereof is finished; and although a remedy is given for this inequality by the sixteenth section of the act of incorporation, which provides, " that the company may increase the toll, if it should appear that the clear profits and income will not bear a dividend of six per centum per annum on the whole capital stock of the company expended, in such manner that the tolls will raise the dividend to six per centum per annum through the whole length of the canal and navigation, and in proportion for each separate part thereof;" yet this remedy cannot be applied to any particular part, till at the end of two years after the whole of the said canal and navigation shall be compleated. Your memorialists are, therefore, instructed by the stockholders further to pray, and they do *pray, That* the Legislature will grant such toll per mile, for any part of the canal that may be finished, as is allowed on the Delaware and Schuylkill canal, under the same restrictions, for that part of the canal so finished, as are provided in the said sixteenth section of the act of incorporation, on the finishing of the whole canal.

By order and in behalf of the corporation,

ROBERT MORRIS, *President*.

To the President, Managers and Company of the Schuylkill and Susquehanna Navigation:

The report of William Weston, Esq. Engineer and Superintendant, &c.

Gentlemen,

PURSUANT to an order of the Board, made in April last, I have now the honor to lay before you, a plan and estimate of that part of the Schuylkill and Susquehanna canal, which extends from the east end of the summit level, to the junction of the Tulpehocken with the river Schuylkill near Reading. Independent of other circumstances, I purposely delayed the survey of the intended line until autumn, as by that means I had an opportunity of viewing the creek in its lowest state. My instructions directed me to explore the Tulpehocken, the adjacent ground, and any other practicable course by which a navigable canal might be made to the Schuylkill. I had conceived very sanguine hopes in favor of the practicability of the latter mode; as I had been informed by persons well acquainted with the face of the country, that there was a probability of finding a more direct route to the Schuylkill, than by following the circuitous windings of the Tulpehocken. But on a very attentive view I do not hesitate to declare that it is impracticable to deviate from the course of the creek; which from its *source* to its *mouth* is environed with hills, so as to render it impossible to leave its banks at any considerable distance, as will be seen by an inspection of the plan. *One* of the two remaining modes must therefore be adopted, viz. a canal navigation totally unconnected with the river: or by using the bed of the present creeks and making such improvements as they are capable of. I have well considered every argument that has been advanced in favor of, and every objection that has been made against, the latter mode. After stating with as much perspicuity as I am able, the reasons that have influenced my determination, I shall leave it to the Board to adopt that plan, which to them appears the most eligible. The contest between river navigations and canals is an old one. Many very plausible arguments have been adduced in favor of the former, and until *time* had proved their fallacy they had much weight, as may be conceived from the many fruitless attempts that have been made in England to render navigable the river Avon, from Stratford to Tewksbury, the Stour to the Severn, the Severn from Shrewsbury to Worcester; the Irwel, the Kennet, the Mersey and the Thames from Crechlade to the tide water; the last of which rivers has employed the abilities of the first engineers for more than a century to no purpose; for after immense sums have been expended upon it, it is now so imperfect as to be unnavigable six months in the year. A collateral canal has been recommended as much cheaper, but the prejudices of corporations, millers and land-owners has hitherto prevented the adoption of this plan. The unerring test of experience has at length convinced the warmest advocates for river navigations how inefficacious they are. I have mentioned the above instances, as practical examples are more conclusive than theoretical arguments. It should also be remembered that the danger to be encountered

tered in this country is much greater than in England, as the floods are more violent and accompanied by ice in greater quantities. The usual method of making rivers navigable is to throw dams acrofs the ftream in the moft convenient fituations, and to build a lock in a collateral channel to enable the boats to pafs from one *pond* to the other. To obtain the neceffary depth of water, the bed of the river at the tail of each lock muft be deepened; or the water raifed fo much by the next dam as to effect the fame purpofe. In the inftance before us the former mode may be deemed impracticable, the bed of the creek being chiefly folid work—The latter is liable to the following objections. To obtain the requifite depth, the water will be raifed higher than the adjacent meadows; to prevent their being overflowed an embankment muft be made which obftructs the natural drainage from the meadows. This may be remedied by cutting a back drain to the tail of the next lock, but, in many inftances, it will be impracticable. Thefe banks are liable to be deftroyed every winter by the floods if raifed only to the height neceffary to *pen* up the water, as they will not be fufficient to confine the river in its bed at that time: and if it overflows it will inevitably deftroy them. To prevent this it follows, that the banks fhould be raifed fufficiently high, and of a proper ftrength, to refift every effort of this powerful element. I am not fo well acquainted with the ftate of the Tulpehocken in the winter feafon as to affign the juft dimenfions of thefe embankments, which will vary with the increafe of its ftream by every new acceffion of water. But from the beft information which I have been able to collect, I have reafon to believe they will deftroy as much land and be nearly as expenfive as cutting a canal. And when every precaution has been taken that human ingenuity can fuggeft they are in continual danger of being deftroyed—and that thefe inftances are far from being rare, the works on the rivers I have beforementioned will evince, having been frequently fwept away. The *lifts* of the locks on the canal will be on an average feven feet; but on the river it would not be prudent to make them more than four or five feet: this circumftance by increafing the number of locks will add confiderably to the expenfe of execution, as the difference between a four feet and feven feet lock is not fo much as may be imagined. For the eafe and conveniencies of hauling, and alfo for its ftability, a towing path fhould be as little elevated above the furface of the water as poffible; but as in the moft favorable feafons the water will be continually fluctuating, it would be neceffary to raife it at leaft three times its ufual height; and then it will be confiderably damaged every flood—If the Tulpehocken was in a permanent ftate it would be much lefs difficult to render it navigable; but its variations both from natural and artificial caufes being fo great, it will be almoft impoffible to affign a juft proportion of *fall* and *lockage*, to acquire the oppofite advantages requifite in a fummer and winter feafon. The above are the moft material objections that occur to me at prefent. The only argument advanced in favor of river navigations is that they are lefs expenfive in the execution. What the *faving* may amount to in the cafe before us is difficult to afcertain; but it will not be of any confequence when put in competition with the manifeft advantages of a canal navigation—And the neceffary annual repairs will, I am perfuaded, amount to as much as the intereft of the principal fum, faved in the execution. As far as my opinion will influence the Board, it is neceffary to declare, that taking every object into confideration, I recommend, as moft fubfervient to their immediate intereft, and

beneficial

beneficial to the public at large, the adoption of a canal navigation, independent of the Tulpehocken, except in such instances as nature, or art, render it expedient to deviate therefrom. These particular cases will be pointed out in the course of the annexed description of the proposed line. Having done my duty, by declaring my opinion, it only remains for me to assure the Board, that whatever their decision may be, I shall execute their orders with as much alacrity as if my recommendation had been adopted.

The *plan* herewith exhibited will give the Board a better information respecting the appearance of the country, the direction of the canal, and the course of the Tulpehocken, than could be conveyed by words. The track of the canal is shewn by a *red* line, and though I may hereafter find it expedient to vary therefrom, in some few instances, these variations will be so trifling as not to cause any sensible alteration in the plan.

The water courses intended to convey the several springs into the summit level of the canal, are distinguished by different colours, which the *table of reference* on the plan will explain. In placing the locks, particular regard has been paid to their *situation* and *lift*, so as to combine the double advantage of suiting the ground, and affording the easiest communication with the divided lands by bridges over the tails, which saves *two hundred* pounds in every instance. In a first survey it cannot be expected that every local circumstance can be comprehended—I may hereafter see sufficient reasons to induce me to make some alteration in their situation and lift; whenever that is done, it will be from economical motives. The ground in Loy's plantation would have admitted the lifts of the locks to have been *ten* feet, but as it would have caused a considerable additional expenditure of water, I have deemed it most eligible to fix them at *six feet*; and this has been continued until additional supplies of water have justified increasing the falls of the subsequent locks.

The regular and uniform descent of the ground in the vicinity of the Tulpehocken prevents us having locks of more than eight feet fall; as the extra digging at the tail of each lock would be more expensive than the saving of an increased lift. On account of the proximity of the hills on each side of the Tulpehocken, the canal is obliged to keep very near the channel, and consequently in the meadows; this circumstance makes it very unpopular with the farmers; but it cannot be avoided, as any other course would enhance the expense of execution infinitely more, than any consideration which will be made for the land. In the following estimate I have been as particular and accurate as the uncertainty of works of this kind will admit. I trust it will be found that sufficient allowance has been made for the execution. In some instances I may have overrated, and in others undervalued the contingent expense; but I believe the average will be found very near what I have allowed it. Not to depend altogether upon appearances to form a judgment of the quality of the ground through which the canal passes, I caused it to be bored in every field—I found the strata generally the same, viz. black earth, clay of different kinds, gravel and rock, on which the borings mostly terminated, but at irregular depths from the surface, viz. from one to six feet. The rock in general lies sufficiently deep from the surface to permit the canal to be cut without interfering with it. When it lies near the surface, I shall cause it to be accurately examined before the canal is set out, and shall regulate the locks accordingly.—It has been a common complaint, (and experience in general has evinced the justice of it) that the estimates of most public works have fallen considerably short of the sums afterwards actually expended in their execution. Whatever may have been the motives for these deceptions, they have not influenced me. The following estimate, (though not greater than the majority of the English canals of the same length have cost) would not have been so high but for the unusual quantity of lockage, and the peculiar disadvantages it labors under in being far removed from most of the necessary materials, particularly stone and sand. However the execution will be as economical as possible, as I shall let all the work by contract that can be done with propriety.

The important article of lockage, I am well persuaded, will be found accurate.—Bridges, the next object, I am not so confident of, with respect to number. I have allowed them in all places where I suppose them necessary, but perhaps a jury may think otherwise. It would be adviseable, in many cases, for the company to purchase the land cut off by the canal, as it is very rarely worth the expense of erecting a bridge, and very frequently not a fourth part. These parcels of land if purchased and re-sold to the owners of the adjacent plantations would save some thousand pounds. In the estimate, I have not included the value of the land necessarily destroyed by the canal; this rests entirely with the juries who have hitherto differed so much in their valuations that no certain idea can be formed of it—In the article of fencing there would be a considerable saving by introducing the modern mode of towing path gates, at the division of every inclosure.

The following description of the nature of the ground through which the canal passes, aided by a reference to the plan, will convey as just an idea of it as can be obtained by any other mode than ocular observation—Beginning at the line of Michael Loy the summit level is continued twenty-two perches to the head of the first lock, between which, and Michael Loy's road, there will be six other locks, of six feet fall each; at the tail of the seventh lock we shall acquire a considerable accession of water by taking in two copious streams which rise in the spring houses of Loy, and Spangler; from this place, therefore, the canal may be considered as abundantly supplied with water at all seasons. Leaving Leonard Immels and Michael Ramlers on the south, the canal passes through the meadows to the west end of Bafsler's milldam, across which an embankment must be made for a towing path three hundred and twenty yards in length, with a waste wear under it to discharge the superfluous water into the mill-pond.

The tenth lock is intended to be placed at the road from Myers town to Lebanon, with a bridge over the tail. Leaving Myers-town about a quarter of a mile to the northward, the canal passes through the lands of Simon Bafsler, and John Myers, to Valentine Millers, in very favorable ground; from thence to the line of John Kufter is one continued rock in length forty perches: this part will be very expensive; I have considered it in the estimate as cut through the solid rock, but if on trial it should prove difficult to quarry, I shall bank over it as the cheapest mode. Through the plantations of Kufter, Haag, Kreitzer and Wolborn the ground in general is good.

Through Sharf's plantation it will be rocky, but, by adapting the fall of the preceding lock to suit the level of the ground, it may in a great measure be avoided. Near the great spring the Tulpehocken makes a considerable elbow, as will be seen by the plan; the canal is laid down as crossing the isthmus. Of the propriety of this route I am not fully satisfied; the distance does not exceed twenty-two perches, but it is composed wholly of rocks in distinct but large masses. To cut the canal through these, and also a new channel for the Tulpehocken, will certainly be very expensive. The next mode of execution is to carry the canal over the Tulpehocken by means of two small aqueducts, and to bank across the isthmus; another mode is to make use of the bed of the river, which may be rendered navigable by erecting a dam at the second intersection, sufficient to raise the water to the requisite height. The first plan is the most perfect, and the last most economical. I am not now prepared to speak decisively on this point; but before it is set out, I shall carefully examine the ground, and adopt that mode which shall appear most eligible. From the great spring, no material obstacle occurs till we arrive at Lower's mill-dam. Here there are two routs, the first through the hill to the northward of the mill, the other by an embankment through the dam; this last is the most preferable, as being much the cheapest. In the estimate I have divided the canal into five districts, the first of which terminates at this place. The length is six miles, four furlongs, and six chains, and the fall one hundred and nine feet seven inches. From Lower's to Lechner's mill, the ground is various in quality, but in general it is not unfavorable. In many places it will be necessary to cut a new channel for the river, as it frequently runs so near the hills as not to leave a sufficient width for a canal and towing path; it will be unnecessary to specify these instances particularly, as they will be shewn more plainly on the plan, where they are denoted by a blue line. At Lechner's, the canal will pass through the hill between the mill and a small out building; at this place I propose to contract the width of the canal to eleven feet, admitting the passage of one boat only at a time; the length of this hill is twenty perches. From Lechner's the canal passes through the plantations of Lantz, Read, Kortz, Brown, Sheafer and Meyer, in favorable ground. The course of the canal through Debe's meadow might have been more direct; but as the circuitous tract, laid down on the plan, saves a bridge, it will be the cheapest. At Edge's it will be advisable to make use of the present dam; indeed there is no alternative, as the hill on the west side, approaching nearly perpendicular to the water edge, precludes every idea of making a canal in this place. All that is necessary here will be to make a towing path elevated about three feet above the surface of the water, that being the height to which the floods generally rise in the winter season. This is the end of the second district, which is five miles, seven furlongs and two chains in length; and the fall is fifty-four feet, eleven inches, divided into eight locks. Leaving the mill-dam by the new race cut to the slitting mill, the canal passes through the plantations of George Ege, Deppe, Lutz and Clinger to Forrar's mill. From this place to the North hill creek, the ground is very irregular in quality. In the wood belonging to Jasper Stump, the canal crosses the North hill; at the time I viewed it, the stream was very trifling, but from the appearance of its banks and the width of the channel, it must be very considerable in the winter season. Until I am better acquainted with it I cannot determine upon the most eligible mode

of

of crossing it, whether by an aqueduct or a tumbling dam. The latter will be the cheapest, but the most inconvenient for the boats. The third district terminates here; the length is six miles and seven furlongs; and the fall forty-eight feet, eight inches, which I have divided into six locks. From hence the canal passes through the plantations of Shomo, Stouch, Geis, and Dunder, to Stouch's mill. From this place to Hiester's mill the ground is various in quality and irregular in surface; a considerable portion is rock, the particulars of which will be specified in the estimate. From Hiester's mill to Raebar's, the canal proceeds in very favorable ground: at this place the river must be turned from its natural course, which will be occupied by the canal. From Raeber's the line of the canal runs through the plantations of Bon, Ruhl, John Raeber, to Read's mill, near which the fortieth lock is placed. From Read's mill to the Schuylkill, the ground on each side of the Tulpehocken, with very few exceptions, is so extremely irregular and rocky, that on account of the enormous expense that would be incident to a canal navigation, it will be the most eligible mode to make the Tulpehocken navigable by means of dams and side locks—The ground on each side of the creek is well adapted to this purpose; in most places it will require no banking, nature having already performed that office; and in those places where the water will be raised above the surface of the adjacent land, it is of so little value as to render the purchase of it an object of little importance—The length of this district, extending from Hiester's mill to the Schuylkill, is eight miles, seven furlongs and four chains, and the fall sixty seven feet, eleven inches.—The total length of the canal, from the east end of the summit level to the Schuylkill, is thirty-four miles, one furlong and six chains; the fall three hundred and ten feet, divided into forty-five locks.

I have the honor to be,

Gentlemen,

Your most obedient humble servant,

WILLIAM WESTON.

January 15*th.* 1794.

(57)

General estimate of the probable cost of compleating the canal from Schuylkill to Susquehanna.

For the crown level from near Lebanon to Michael Loy's, nearly compleated, upwards of three miles, - - £. 40,000 0 0

	Length.		Fall.				
	Mis. furlng.		feet. inch.				
From the summit to Lower's mill,	6	4, 6	109	7	£. 54,233	0	11¼
Lower's to Ege's,	5	7, 2	54	11	30,575	7	1¼
Ege's to the North-hill,	6	7, 0	48	8	30,819	2	3
North-hill to Hiester's,	5	7, 4	28	11	26,848	10	3¼
Hiester's to the Schuykill,	8	7, 4	67	11	43,894	15	6¼
	34	1, 6	310	0	£. 186,373	16	2

Cost of land already valued, - - - 8,051 0 0
Cost of land necessary on the same estimate, - - 15,300 0 0
Ten houses for clerks and toll gatherers, - - 1,500 0 0
Supposed damages to lands, mills, water, &c. - 4,700 0 0
Salaries, office-hire and incidental charges for all persons employed by the company for four years, - - - 10,078 3 10

Whole cost from Lebanon to Schuylkill, thirty-eight miles, average £. 7000 per mile, - - - 266,000 0 0
From Lebanon to Susquehanna the difficulty will not be so great—thirty-two miles supposed to cost £. 6000 per mile, - 192,000 0 0

Total valuation, - - - £. 458,000 0 0
Sum provided for by law, 1000 shares, at 400 dollars, - 150,000 0 0

Deficient and to be provided for, - - - £. 308,000 0 0

One hundred and sixteen thousand pounds, a part of the sum deficient, will complete the work from Lebanon to Schuylkill; when that part is finished the company will draw a considerable annual toll. The citizens of the state will be convinced that although this great work will be attended with considerable difficulty, it can be surmounted so as to perfect a navigation from the eastern to the western waters. For finishing the work from Lebanon to Susquehanna a further sum of £. 192,000 is to be provided, making agreeably to the above estimate, £. 308,000

But as the work from Lebanon to Susquehanna has not yet been laid out by the engineer, £. 192,000 is mentioned as the greatest sum, supposing no part of the bed of the Quittapahilla and Swatara to be made use of. But if, instead of a canal navigation along the whole margin of the rivers, the beds of the said rivers, wherever they can be made safe and permanent, should be adopted, the expense may possibly be found less. This point will be ascertained during the ensuing Summer.

P   *Report*

Report of WILLIAM WESTON, *Esquire, for the Year* 1794.

To the PRESIDENT and MANAGERS of the *Schuylkill* and *Sufquehanna* Navigation Companies.

Gentlemen,

HAVING received from the Secretary of the Schuylkill and Sufquehanna canal, the requeſt of the Managers for my immediate attendance on the committee, who are appointed to ſtate the preſent ſituation of their works, and a general ſtatement of their affairs;—I have endeavored to ſupply them with every information which the ſhortneſs of the notice would allow. It was my original intention to have poſtponed my report until the cloſe of the preſent year; but the commands of the Board not permitting me to carry it to that time, I have endeavored to anticipate, as accurately as poſſible, the probable ſtate of the works at that period. It muſt be underſtood, that the annexed details and ſtatements relate only to that part of the canal eaſtward of the ſummit level, the operations of which commenced early in June; the previous expenſe of day-wage, and ſome ſubſequent pieces of contract work on the ſummit, will be included in Mr. Roberdeau's accounts herewith exhibited.

I flatter myſelf the progreſs made in the works, in the ſhort ſpace of ſeven months, will prove ſatisfactory to the Board. On a careful compariſon of the actual ſtate of the various works, and an ample allowance for the completion of ſuch parts as remain unfiniſhed, with the previous eſtimate laid before the Board in my laſt report, it appears, that from the eaſt end of the ſummit level to Michael Kreitzer's plantation, a diſtance of more than four miles and a quarter, the actual expenditure will fall ſhort of the eſtimated one at leaſt *three thouſand pounds*. Though I would not wiſh to appear too ſanguine, yet I may be allowed to draw favorable inferences of the remainder of the line; which, if realized, cannot be more gratifying to the Board than pleaſing to myſelf.—Independant of this, I have well-founded reaſons for aſſerting, that the works will rather proportionably diminiſh than increaſe in expenſe, as the important object of land-carriage will, after the enſuing year, in a great meaſure be done away, by the canal being made ſubſervient to that purpoſe. The ſand for the locks, bridges, &c. will be (from the approaching proximity of the canal) delivered at the reſpective works for little more than half the preſent coſt; the ſame remark will hold good reſpecting the lime. Though the average value of the bricks (reduced to ſtatute ſize) will not exceed twenty-four ſhillings per thouſand, yet I muſt own I have been diſappointed in the *quantity* made the laſt ſeaſon; the unfavorable ſtate of the weather, during the greateſt part of the ſummer, has prevented the produce coming up to my calculations; at the ſame time that the number has been diminiſhed, the coſt of thoſe actually made has of conſequence been increaſed. From the difficulty of procuring waggons to haul bricks, lime, ſand, &c. I was under the

neceſſity

neceffity of not employing half the number of bricklayers I had at firſt contemplated; though, at the fame time, more work has been done in *four months* than is generally executed on moſt canals in one *feafon*. Five locks of ſix feet fall, and two road bridges, are compleated, and fuch progreſs made in the fixth lock, and two more bridges, that a fortnight's work, in the enſuing ſpring, will ſuffice to finiſh them. The whole of the works on the canal (excepting ſuch parts as it would have been imprudent to fet) have been executed by contract, and on ſuch terms as I doubt not will be fatisfactory to the Board. As the ſubſequent ſtatements contain the whole of the expenſes incurred on the reſpective articles to the preſent period, it is proper to obſerve that a confiderable portion thereof belongs to the next year's account;— upwards of a *million and a half* of *bricks*; *holiow quoins* for *ten locks*; *coping* for *nine* bridges; and a confiderable quantity of lime, fand, &c. are now on hand, ready for immediate uſe. The different works are claſſed feparately; the amount of theſe will not contain the whole expenſes of the preſent year; there being many accounts which could not with propriety be fixed to any article, others that belong not ſolely to the preſent year, and others which I have had no opportunity of feeing; but the accounts of Mr. Roberdeau and Mr. Beatty will give the Board every information they may deſire on this head.

      I am, Gentlemen,
        With the greateſt reſpect,
         Your obedient humble ſervant,
          WILLIAM WESTON.

Lebanon, December 16*th.* 1794.

Account of the number of bricks made for the uſe of the Schuylkill and Suſquehanna canal, and the attendant expenſe.

	£	s	d
Digging of clay, 9785 cubic yards at 6*d*. 7*d*. and 8*d*. per yard,	294	2	2
Moulding and burning,	1418	17	9
Tempering and ditto,	1042	12	6
Wheeling and ditto,	724	3	5
Off bearing,	346	6	5
Wood-cutting, 2388 cord of wood at 2/6, 3/ and 3/9 per cord	358	11	10½
Labour of various kinds—emptying kilns, ſtacking the bricks, &c.	622	0	0
Hauling wood, fand, duſt, &c.	391	19	1
Amount carried over, £.	5198	13	2¼

Amount brought forward, £. 5198 13 2¼

998,699 bricks laid in the locks and bridges.
72,065 ditto laid in the stop-gate, towing-path, walls, &c.
1,419,236 ditto in the brick-yard.
106,000 ditto at the sixth lock.
204,000 ditto in kilns, clamps, chimneys, &c.
─────────
2,800,000 Total, which reduced to statute size, and some deductions made which do not belong to the brick account, will average twenty-four shillings per thousand.

Brick-laying.

Laying 1,103,052 bricks in the five locks, bridges, &c. - 987 19 4

Lime.

Burning 10¼ kilns of lime, at £.12 12*s* per kiln, £.134 8 0
Cutting wood and hauling, - - , 99 5 11
─────────
233 13 11

7500 bushels of lime, which is equivalent to 7¼ per bushel,

Sand.

Damages of land by digging, unbasing the sand pit, digging and loading the sand, and hauling ditto to the locks and bridges, - 281 16 4
Three hundred and sixty waggon loads have been delivered at the locks and bridges, containing fourteen thousand four hundred bushels, equal to four pence half penny per bushel.

£.6702 2 6

Cutting the Canal from the east end of the summit to Kreitzer's.

Length—4 miles, 16½ chains, Amount, £.8526 13 2; viz.

	Chains.	Links.				
Through Loy's plantation,	46	25	-	-	876	7 3
Spangler's ditto, . -	20	51	-	-	369	11 8
Immel's ditto, - -	22	86	-	-	616	17 2
M. Rambler's ditto, -	23	60	-	-	645	12 2
L. Rambler's ditto, -	16	50	-	-	498	6 9
T. Basler's ditto, -	39	40	-	-	710	7 11
Myer's ditto, -	41	50	-	-	1353	11 10
S. Basler's ditto, - -	18	50	-	-	522	6 4
Miller's ditto, - -	27	10	-	-	931	9 9
Kushter's ditto, -	19	40	-	-	606	0 0
Haag's ditto, -	30	90	-	-	746	9 8
Kreitzer's ditto, -	30		-	-	649	13 8

Total £. 8526 13 2

Amount brought forward, £. 8526 13 2

Stone-work.

	£. s. d.	£. s. d.
Getting stone at the different quarries for the locks and bridges,	£.761 7 6	
Hauling stone from the quarries to the canal,	189 15 0	
Working and setting the coping of the bridges, hollow quoins of the locks,	424 15 0	
		1375 17 6

Waggons.

	£. s. d.	£. s. d.
Hauling bricks, lime, &c. from May 19th. to December 31st.	£.186 4 7	
Feed for the company's horses, overseers' and waggoners' wages,	597 7 6	
		783 12 1

Lock-pits.

	£. s. d.	£. s. d.
By order in favor of Samuel Galbraith for cutting 1st. lock-pit,	£. 56 1 3	
Ditto ditto ditto 2d. ditto,	48 17 6	
Ditto ditto ditto 3d. ditto,	48 17 6	
Ditto ditto ditto 4th. ditto,	48 17 6	
Ditto ditto James Rannels 5th. ditto,	137 16 6	
Ditto ditto Samuel Galbraith 6th. ditto,	262 6 3	
Ditto ditto John Fletcher 7th. ditto,	97 17 9	
Ditto ditto John Butler 8th. ditto,	120 0 0	
Ditto ditto Thomas Morris 9th. ditto,	72 7 6	
		993 1 9
Backing the five locks in Michael Loy's wood to December 31st.		465 5 0
		£. 12134 9 6

December 15th. 1794.

A comparative statement *of the expense of conveying* twenty tons *of produce from Middle-town, on the Susquehanna, to the city of Philadelphia, by* LAND *and by* WATER *carriage.*

Water-carriage.

	Miles.
Schuylkill and Susquehanna canal, say	70
Schuylkill, from Reading to Norristown, - - -	46
Schuylkill and Delaware canal, -	16
	132

	£	s	d
Toll on 20 tons of produce for * 86 miles of canal navigation, at 1/16 of a dollar per mile, £.40	6	3	
Hauling 20 tons { 1 man 5 days,	1	5	0
132 miles, - { 1 boy 5 days,	1	0	0
{ 1 horse 5 days,	1	10	0
Freight or hire of a boat,	0	18	9
20 tons for £.45	0	0	
Or £.2 5 0 per ton,			
Or 0 3 11¼ per barrel of flour, -			
Or 0 1 2¼ per bushel of wheat, -			

The above produce is conveyed to market by 2 men, 1 horse.

Land-carriage.

	Miles.
From Middle-town to Philadelphia,	100

The *present* price of carriage from Middle-town to Philadelphia is 5/6 per *cwt.* or for 20 tons - £.110 0 0

Or £.5 10 0 per ton.
Or 0 9 7¼ per barrel of flour.
Or 0 2 11¼ per bushel of wheat.

The same by land requires 20 men, 18 horses.

AN ATTEMPT *to ascertain the probable trade and consequent tonnage on the* Schuylkill *and* Susquehanna CANAL, [*as referred to in the note at the bottom of page iv of the Introduction.*]

I. Taking the extent of country on an average width of 10 miles on each side of the canal from *Reading* to *Middletown*, the distance being 55 miles by a straight course, we shall have 1100 square miles, or 704,000 acres; and taking each plantation at 320 acres, we have 2200 plantations. Supposing each plantation to cultivate 40 acres of grain, at 10 bushels per acre, the total produce will amount to 880,000 bushels, which, at 60*lb.* per bushel, gives 23,576 tons; and taking the average tonnage at half the length of the canal, or 35 miles, according to its various windings, it amounts to, at one sixteenth of a dollar per ton per mile, £.19351 19 4

Sum carried over, £.19351 19 4

---

* N. B. Forty-six miles from Reading to Norris-town, where the bed of the Schuylkill is to be used as a temporary navigation, being taken from the whole distance of 132 miles, leave 86 miles as above, for the canal navigation subject to tolls.

(63)

Sum brought forward, £. 19351 19 4

II. The produce of the extensive country bordering on the navigable waters of the Susquehanna and its numerous branches, are at present very great; but in a few years, from the natural increase of population, it will be so immense as to exceed the bounds of calculation; at present we believe it may very safely be estimated at 600,000 bushels or 16,071 tons, and as the distance is 70 miles, the tonnage will amount to £. 1 12 9¼ per ton,   26366 9 8

III. Back carriage, consisting of *salt, groceries, liquors,* and various kinds of European and domestic manufactures; this we will estimate at *one fourth* of the above, or   11429 12 3

IV. The carriage of *lime, timber* for building, *coals, fire-wood, iron, stone, bricks,* &c. will certainly be very great; but such as to render it impossible to form an accurate idea of the amount; but taking it at the lowest rate it may be estimated at *one eighth* of the two first articles,   5714 16 1¼

    £. 62862 17 4½

Exclusive of the above annual income, the stockholders will derive great emolument from the seats for water works, of which there will be many from the surplus water at the different locks within the grounds purchased for the canal, and without damage to the mills erected on the lands of the adjoining owners. It will also be a peculiar advantage, that from the situation of these water-works, all produce and manufactures, or raw materials, may be loaded or unloaded directly, without the intervention of land carriage, to and from the boats. The waters of the Tulpehocken and Quittapahilla are abundantly copious to supply every demand for any purpose of this kind whatever. The above calculation, at a dividend of 12 per cent. per annum, is equal to a capital of £. 523,850; but, calculating the most moderate increase of population, the toll will increase, even on this capital, one per cent. per annum; until it amounts to the limitation, in the act of incorporation, and then the toll will be subject to a reduction according to law.

Delaware

(64)

Delaware and Schuylkill Canal.

This Canal is intended to anſwer the double purpoſe of forming a capital link in the great chain of weſtern navigation, from the Ohio and lake Erie to Philadelphia, as well as for an abundant ſupply of wholeſome water to all parts of the city. The canal will connect the navigation of the Schuylkill with the Delaware, and is carried on a level of 49 feet above the high water mark of the Delaware, for about 16 miles to Broad ſtreet; and from thence is conducted into the Delaware above Callow Hill-ſtreet, through ſix locks, the diſtance being about one mile. The report of the deputy engineer ſtates, that * one third of the work is finiſhed, and that contracts are formed and forming for a vigorous proſecution during the preſent year; and the committee with confidence can aſſert, that a proper attention of the ſtockholders to the punctual payment of the monies when called for by the Preſident and Managers, will enable the Board to draw a toll for part of the diſtance in the year 1796, and to compleat the whole in three or four years.

The following eſtimate of revenue the ſtockholders may, with ſafety, calculate on when the work is completed.

All the produce paſſing through the upper canal, and ſupplies returning muſt paſs through this canal; the eſtimate of the Suſquehanna and Schuylkill canal is fixed at £. 62,862 for 35 miles; the Delaware and Schuylkill draw the ſame toll per mile in proportion to the diſtance, which will amount to - - - £. 31,431 0 0

The probable toll, from the produce of the lands bordering on the Schuylkill and waters thereof, not eſtimated in the above, will at leaſt produce one half the amount, - - 15,715 0 0

The canal paſſing for about 5 miles through a variety of marble free ſtone and lime ſtone quarries, from which the city is ſupplied with materials for building and ornament, will, by calculating the number of waggons now employed in tranſporting thoſe materials to the city, produce at leaſt - - - 15,000 0 0

Total £. 62,146 0 0

---

* By a rough calculation, which is by no means exaggerated, I find we have blaſted with powder and quarried, five millions four hundred and forty five thouſand cubic feet of rock, and have mounded up, between the towing path of the canal and the river, a bank with the ſtone and rubbiſh, from 20 to 25 feet high from its baſe in the river. We have made at our brickyard, laſt ſummer, about three hundred thouſand bricks.
At the lower end of the canal, in the vicinity of the city, through the diſtance of two miles and three quarters, there have been two hundred and fifty thouſand cubic yards of earth and gravel and partly rocks, removed out of the bed of the canal, and ten culverts built and complicated.

The stock of the company, as already subscribed, amounts to £. 150000, which, from the costs of that part of the canal already cut, will be sufficient for the completion of the work necessary for the transportation of produce; the toll of which will amount, agreeably to the foregoing estimate, to £. 62000 per annum, making a dividend of upwards of forty-one per cent. but, agreeably to the charter granted to the company, the toll is to be so reduced every ten years, as not to afford more than a dividend of 25 per cent. per annum.

In addition to the £. 150000 subscribed, a further sum of about £. 50000 will be wanting to complete the watering of the city, on which the stockholders, by law, are allowed a further dividend of 10 per cent. per annum. This great object is of such immense consequence to the health of the city, and to the extinguishing of fires, that the citizens of Philadelphia will cheerfully pay, for the use of the water, a sum more than adequate to the payment of the 10 per cent. allowed by law.

In addition to the advantages already stated, great revenues may be drawn from the application of the surplus water passing through the canal, which, from Broad-street to the Delaware, affords a fall of near 50 feet. Dry docks are, also, contemplated by the law, and will, when the resources of the company become ample, be carried into effect.

Respecting the dimensions of this canal, it has been determined:

1st. That the width of the bottom be twenty feet.

2d. That the depth of water be three feet and an half.

3d. That the width of the canal be thirty feet and an half.

4th. That the width of the towing path be ten feet.

5th. That the towing path be not less than one foot above the surface of the water in any place.

6th. That the locks be constructed to admit boats of sixty feet in length and nine feet in width.

7th. That the descent of the canal be at the rate of two inches per mile.

(N. B. The new river canal, for conducting water to the city of London, has three inches descent per mile, but this has been found more than necessary, and increases the expense of maintaining the bank.)

On the petition of the President and Managers of the *Schuylkill* and *Susquehanna* canal company, the Legislature have been pleased to pass the following supplement:—

A supplement to an act, entitled, " An act to enable the Governor of this commonwealth to incorporate a company, for opening a canal and lock navigation between the rivers Schuylkill and Susquehanna, by the waters of Tulpehocken, Quittapahilla and Swatara, in the counties of Berks and Dauphin."

Section I. *Be it enacted by the Senate and House of Representatives of the commonwealth of Pennsylvania, in General Assembly met, and it is hereby enacted by the authority of the same,* That it shall and may be lawful for the President, Managers and Company of the Schuylkill and Susquehanna navigation, when any part of the said canal and lock navigation shall be in use, to demand and receive of and from the persons having the charge of all boats and vessels, rafts of timber, boards, plank or scantling, passing through the said canal and navigation, and the locks thereunto belonging, at the rate of one sixteenth of a dollar, by the mile, for every ton weight of the burthen of said boats and vessels, to be ascertained as provided for in the act to which this is a supplement, and in like manner one sixteenth of a dollar, by the mile, for every hundred feet, cubic measure, of boards or timber, and the same sum, by the mile, for twelve hundred feet, board measure, of boards, plank or scantling in rafts, and in proportion for rafts of a greater or less size.

Section II. *And be it further enacted by the authority aforesaid,* That it shall and may be lawful, to and for the said President, Managers and Company, to open a subscription, for such additional number of shares, in such manner, and at such times, as they may judge necessary, to complete the said canal and lock navigation.

Section III. *And be it further enacted by the authority aforesaid,* That it shall and may be lawful, to and for the said President, Managers and Company, if they shall think it necessary and for the interest of the said company, to negociate and borrow, upon the credit of their capital stock and incorporation, and the tolls and profits of the same, such sum or sums of money, from time to time, as they may be able to procure, and shall deem expedient and necessary, for carrying on and compleating the said work.

GEORGE LATIMER, *Speaker of the House of Representatives.*

WILLIAM BINGHAM, *Speaker of the Senate.*

Approved, February the twelfth, 1795.

THOMAS MIFFLIN, *Governor of the commonwealth of Pennsylvania.*

APPENDIX.

APPENDIX.

IN a *historical* view, according to the order of *time*, the following papers shoul[d] have been inserted immediately after page 47 of the preceding sheets. As soon as the *subscriptions* were compleated, and the several canal companies organized by an election of a President, Managers and other officers; committees were appointed to lay off and level the proposed tracts of the *canals*, and to report to the Boards of Managers.

The summit level, or middle ground, between the head waters of Quittapahilla near Lebanon, and those of Tulpehockon near Myer's town, (a distance of about four miles and a half) had been examined and levelled, about twenty five years ago, by a committee appointed by the *American Philosophical Society*, viz. *William Smith*, D. D. then Provost of the college of Philadelphia, *John Lukens*, Esquire, Surveyor General of the province (now state) of Pennsylvania, and *John Sellers*, Esquire. The same ground was afterwards examined and levelled, under legislative sanction, by sundry skilful persons, and among others by the celebrated philosopher and mechanic *David Rittenhouse*, Esquire, L. L. D. his brother *Benjamin Rittenhouse*, *Timothy Matlack*, *John Adlum*, Esquires, and others, all agreeing in the results of their work, respecting the proper tract of the canal, for a junction of the Schuylkill and Susquehanna;—extending their prospects still further to the great plan now in operation, viz. the junction of the tide-waters of Delaware with the Ohio and western lakes. But the dark and distressing period of the revolution necessarily suspended all improvements of this nature, in every part of America, until the glorious æra of the *peace* and *independence* of the United States, when they were first resumed in the states of Virginia and Maryland, upon the Potomack, under the auspices of the illustrious WASHINGTON, during his short recess from his public labors; next in the state of PENNSYLVANIA, as set forth in the last page of the *Introduction* to these papers; and speedily afterwards, with a noble emulation of public spirit, in most of the other states, according to their natural advantages, as *New York*, *Connecticut*, *Massachusetts*, the *Carolinas*, &c.

The company of the Schuylkill and Susquehanna navigation being (as above mentioned) the first organized in Pennsylvania, a committee, viz. Dr. *Smith* and *Timothy Matlack*, Esquire, were appointed to repair to the summit ground near Lebanon, and finally to re-examine the levels, to ascertain the exact route of the canal, the sources and quantity of the waters which could be brought to supply the reservoir on the summit, and the locks at each end; with an account of the lands and waters necessary to be purchased as the great basis of the work. The same committee were also appointed to level and lay out the *Conewago canal*, and finished their work in July, 1792. A committee was also appointed to lay out and level the *Delaware* and *Schuylkill* canal, from Norris town to Philadelphia, viz. Dr. *Rittenhouse*, Dr. *Smith* and *Samuel Powel*, Esquire. There is a responsibility attached to the companies and their Managers, as well concerning their own diligence as that of their committees, which is the only apo-

* logy

logy for the mention of these appointments. But the President and Managers did not think it proper to depend wholly on their own judgment, or the judgment of their committees, in works of such magnitude and immense public consequence. They, therefore, determined to engage one of the ablest engineers that could be procured from England, to superintend and direct their works; and in the mean while, that there might be no unnecessary delay, they commenced their undertakings at such places, on the three *canals*, as appeared to them to leave no room for the choice of better ground, or for any error which could materially affect the work;—the *Schuylkill* and *Susquehanna* canal under the superintendance of *John Bull*, Esquire, the *Delaware* and *Schuylkill* canal under Mr. *Jonathan Robeson*, and the *Conewago* canal under Mr. *James Brindley*.

Early in the month of January, 1793, arrived from *London* WILLIAM WESTON, Esquire, the *engineer* engaged by the companies; a gentleman who had directed the execution of some of the principal canals in England, whose great abilities, activity and experience in all the branches of his department, have merited and obtained the perfect confidence and esteem of the Managers; and whose advice and assistance, which have been solicited and given as occasion might permit, will be of the utmost importance towards the facilitating improvements of a similar nature in the neighboring states.

After some necessary arrangements with the President and Managers of the several canals, Mr. *Weston*, accompanied by one of the committee who had assisted in laying them out, left Philadelphia February first, and proceeded to that part of the canal begun at Norris town, arriving at Lebanon February fourth. He found more than six hundred men at work, viz. upwards of two hundred at Norris town, and about four hundred at the summit or middle ground, between Lebanon and Myers town. The following *abstract* of his *report* made to the companies on his return, gave them great satisfaction, viz.

"From such a view as the time and the season of the year would permit me to take of the canal through the middle ground near Lebanon, I have little doubt but the most favorable line has been adopted.

"The first and most important object is a due and adequate supply of water. I judged it expedient to examine the various springs which are to supply the summit of the canal, but not with intention to ascertain the quantity they afford (this being an improper season for that purpose) but to view their situation with respect to the summit level. It is very apparent they may be conducted into the canal with great ease. The springs were lower than when gauged last summer. It will be needless to say any thing further on this subject, as Dr. *Smith* will deliver to the committee a calculation of the number of lock-fulls of water they yield in twenty-four hours; which seems to have been made with great care and attention. This I apprehend will be adequate to the trade that may reasonably be supposed to pass over the summit, making proper allowance for exhalation and leekage. Suppose the crown level $3\frac{1}{4}$ miles in length, the extra depth 4 feet, the mean width 32 feet, it will contain 2,365,440 cubic feet of water, which, at 3420 cubic feet to a lock, will give 691 locks full.

" The

"The Delaware and Schuylkill canal appears to be judiciously laid out, by keeping as near the banks of the river as the nature of the ground would admit.

"The fault of this canal, supposing the dimensions perfectly right, as formed by persons intimately acquainted with the state of the waters and the boats navigable on them, I observe to be this, viz. that the proposed depth of water being 3¼ feet, and the width at bottom 20 feet, the surface with the proper slope should have been 30¼ feet, whereas I found it but 27, the angle of the slope being 45 degrees; whereas the present practice is an angle of 33¾ degrees, and the bottom and top as 2 to 3.

"The result of a conference with Dr. *Rittenhouse*, respecting the fall it may be necessary to give the canal, in order to supply the city with water, will be explained to the Board by Dr. *Smith*, together with other matters necessary to be known, but which do not come immediately in my department.

"WILLIAM WESTON."

An abstract of the REPORT *of Dr.* SMITH, *respecting the Schuylkill and Susquehanna canal, so far as above referred to by Mr.* WESTON.

"On Tuesday, February fifth, 1793, I accompanied Mr. *Weston*, from the main body of the *canal* where the workmen were employed, to view the several springs and waters at their sources and heights, from whence they are proposed to be conducted to the canal at the summit level, and where they had been *gauged* by Mr. *Matlack* and myself, as a committee of the company, in July last.

"Mr. *Weston*, in his *Report*, has stated to the *Board* the reasons of our not considering it necessary to make any new estimate of the quantity of those waters, and his present idea of their competency to a full supply of the locks, "adequate to the trade that may be reasonably supposed to pass over the summit, making the proper allowance for *exhalation*, *oozing* and *leakage*." He has examined the calculations, and having given them his sanction, as appearing to have been made with care and accuracy, I now *report* them to be entered among the proceedings of the Board, as materials for the engineer to proceed upon, and to be examined in other states of the water.

Estimate of the waters and springs to supply one locks of the grand canal between the waters of Tulpehocken and Quittapahilla, at the rate of 3420 cubic feet, to be expended in passing a set of locks.

East end.

I.

Kantner's mill stream.

Breadth, Depth, Length in inches. Cub. feet. Time. Cub. ft. pr. day. Locks per day.
48 × 3,96 × 396 = } 75271,68 = 43,61 = in 17″ = $\frac{221641,44}{3420}$ = 64,5 or one lock full in about 22 minutes.

II. *Breckhill's spring and waters*, measured at the road a little below the spring house.

Breadth, Depth, Length. Cub. inches. Cub. feet. Min. Cub. ft. pr. day. Locks per day.
43 × 5,41 × 396 = 92121,48 = 53,31 in 1′ = $\frac{76760,4}{3420}$ = 22,4 or about one lock in 1 hr. 4 min.

III. Baylor's spring, measured at the road below his meadows,—two thirds of the water, which issues from the great spring near his house, being then spread over the meadows or flowing in the water courses.

Breadth, Depth, Length. Cub. inches. Cub. feet. Cub. ft. per day. Locks.
24 × 3,11 × 396 = 29362,4 = 17,65 in 73″ = $\frac{20179,74}{3420}$ = 5,9; but if taken at the spring head, and conducted in pipes or a trunk, without wasting, would yield + 11,8 locks, or 17,7 locks per day.

West end.

Punch spring, measured by making a dam at the spring head.

Breadth, Depth, Length. Cub. inches. Cub. feet. Cub. ft. per day. Locks.
141,6 × 5,38 × 396 = 301675,968 = 174,563 in 8′ = $\frac{31421,34}{3420}$ = 9,33 per day.

Ditto, measured lower down, in the natural channel, without a dam.

Breadth, Depth, Length. Cub. inches. Cub. feet. Cub. ft. per day. Locks.
36,07 × 1,5 × 240 = 12985,2 = 7,514 in 17″ = $\frac{38188,8}{3420}$ = 11,16 per day.

II. Upper Punch spring.

Breadth, Depth, Length. Cub. in. bar. Cub. feet. Cub. ft. per day. Locks.
24 × 1,73 × 396 = 16441,92 = 9,55 in 70″ = $\frac{10787,333}{3420}$ = 3,154 per day.

N. B. The measurement where the dam was first made, being the lowest, it is probable that the water had not risen to flow over the dam at its full height, or to the same height which it had when the water was measured below.

The mean of both will give
$\left.\begin{array}{l}\text{Locks.}\\9,33\\11,16\end{array}\right\}$ Locks. 10,5

III. Martin Light's brook, or run, to be united with the two Punch springs, and carried on the level of the lower Punch spring, to the reservoir.

Measured at a deep and wide place below a ford. } Breadth. Depth. Length. Cub. inches. Cub. feet.
Measured at a shallow & narrow place with greater velocity. } 83,26 × 6,9 × 360 = 221545,656 = 128,2 in 4′ 15″ = $\frac{43436,4}{3420}$ = 12,7 per day.
76,44 × 2,64 × 360 = 72648,576 = 42,042 in 1′ 32″ or 92″ = $\frac{39482,91}{3420}$ = 11,545 p. day. } $\left.\begin{array}{l}\textit{Mean locks}\\\textit{per day.}\\12,122\end{array}\right.$

The amount of the whole is upwards of 130 locks per day, which will ascend and descend 75 boats of from 7 to 40 tons each

"At the season of the year in which these springs and waters were *gauged*, the weather was extremely warm, the evaporation great, and many of them *gauged* after having passed over large meadows. I have therefore no hesitation in declaring, that the quantity given may be safely taken as rather under than above the *mean* quantity, at the driest and warmest times of the year; and I trust this will be verified by Mr. *Weston's* future examinations; and if any deficiency should, upon an increased state of the trade, be found in the quantity of those waters, it may be supplied, as I hinted in a former report, by the introduction of Furnace creek, and even the Swatara and some of its branches; and the increased trade will enable the company to make use of all these auxiliary supplies hen necessary. But, without these, Mr. *Weston's* abilities, even with the present waters, will introduce constructions in the locks, at a small expense, whereby one *third* of the quantity of water in each lock may be saved, exclusive of the *Reservoir* on the summit level, which may be constructed, according to his report, to contain 691 locks full of water, to be accumulated by occasional rains at all seasons of the year, and by the natural supply of the springs on such days as the number of boats, passing the locks, may be short of the number calculated upon, which will probably be the case for a long time to come.

"WILLIAM SMITH.

"*February* 19*th,* 1793."

RECAPITULATION.

MORE than two years have elapsed since the *engineer* delivered his first report, approving the general plan of the works, as projected by the companies, and in considerable progress before his arrival. His experience and labors during that period, have fully justified the accuracy of the calculations, and the easy practicability of all the projections. Upwards of fifteen miles, including the work on both canals, commenced before his arrival, are in general nearly compleated or finished, with the necessary locks, and through the most difficult grounds; a distance of more than four miles and a quarter of which, were finished in about seven months of the last summer and autumn; the actual expenditure on which fell short of the estimated one at least *three* thousand pounds,—yielding a favorable presumption, that, in the progress of the works, the expense will rather be proportionably diminished than increased. [See his reports for 1793 and 1794, particularly the latter, page 58 of the preceding papers.]

Upon the whole, it appears demonstrably evident, that this grand canal navigation (through a course of seventy miles distance, joining the *Schuylkill* at the mouth of Tulpehocken, with *Susquehanna* at the mouth of Swatara, whereby the *carrying trade*, between Philadelphia and the western waters of the *Ohio* and *great lakes*, will be commenced and proceed in operation) may be compleated, on a secure and permanent foundation, for the sum of - - £. 450,000

Bu.

But by the lowest calculation of the trade which may, at present, be expected through this distance of seventy miles (without estimating its immense future increase, by the increase of population, through an extent of country of more than two hundred miles square, whose waters will communicate with this canal) it would yield a dividend of 12 per cent. per annum to the stockholders, which is equal (see page 63) to a capital of £. 523,850

So that there would be a present surplus of a toll of 12 per cent. (increasing annually) equal to a capital of £. 73,850, beyond the capital necessary for compleating the work.

This surplus, with a dividend of 12 per cent. yearly increasing, (setting aside for a moment the incitements of public spirit) is certainly more than sufficient to incite the most active perseverance in the great undertaking, and every effort of the company to increase their capital to the amount, which, as stated above, is - - £. 450,000

Of this sum, the subscriptions of the stockholders, according to the original act of incorporation, amount to - - 150,000

Deficient, about £. 300,000

There are but two ways of supplying this deficiency, as was stated in a memorial to the Legislature, (see page 49) *viz.*

1st. Either by enlarging the present capital by the increase of shares and new subscriptions, on the terms of the act of incorporation; or,

2d. By the company's negociating and obtaining an *effectual loan;* or, perhaps, partly in both these methods.

But by reason of the large sums of money already invested in the various stocks of this state and of the United States, such as banks, insurance companies, *roads*, canal and other companies, and the growing demands of capital for our increased domestic and foreign trade among our monied citizens; there appears but little prospect either of obtaining a *loan* or an increase of shares to any considerable amount among individual capitalists in this country, nor a prompt payment of a considerable number of the shares already subscribed according to law.

And although it might be possible, and perhaps probable, in the present fluctuating state of property among *capitalists* in Europe, to obtain a *foreign loan*, upon the ample prospects, which the magnitude of this undertaking holds forth, of a speedy and secure return, either of the capital, or liberal profits on the footing of stockholders; yet the length of time, and expense attending the *negociation*, would give a damp to the work, and occasion such a stop or suspension of it, as would be dishonorable to the state and fatal in the issue; considered not only as a check to our western population, and a grievous prolongation of the time in which the present stockholders might expect some returns for their money advanced, not to mention the bad policy of vesting such a large proportion as two thirds of the stock and profits of so great an undertaking, in the hands of foreigners; although one *third* might be prudently vested in this way, while the state might hold the other third.

This distribution of the capital into three parts, the *commonwealth* and original stockholders being invested with *two*, would undoubtedly secure the raising of the other third part, upon an advantageous loan, or new subscriptions for shares, either at *home* or *abroad*, and thereby likewise ensure the speedy and compleat success of the work.

The finances of the state are in a flourishing condition; and it is submitted to the wisdom and feelings of an enlightened Legislature, to what nobler purposes they can be applied (in part at least) than to the improvement of our country, and the encouragement of arts and manufactures, even if no monied return were to be expected, on the capital to be expended; for, can an interest of 8 or 10 per cent. on the monied capital of a great commonwealth be considered as an equivalent for suffering the improvements of a happy and fertile country to languish and decay? But when it is considered that even in a monied view, the stock to be vested in the shares of this *canal* will produce a larger and more growing interest or dividend than can be contemplated on any other species of stock, besides the additional interest, in point of revenue, from an increase of population and of the wealth of our citizens, it is hoped the Legislature " who have already put their hands to the *plough* (by the liberal benefactions and grants which are stated below) will not look back," nor suffer their former liberality to be lost to the public, by any abatement of their protection and encouragement.

Grants of public money for the improvement of roads and waters by the Legislature of Pennsylvania.

APPROPRIATION of £. 5000 (part of £. 10,000 appropriated by a former act for claims and improvements) yearly.

A sum, not exceeding £. 2500, shall be expended and laid out, under the direction of Council, for clearing and making navigable certain parts of the river Susquehanna, above Wright's ferry and the Juniata, and their waters, &c. *viz.*

£.1000 for clearing and making navigable the Schuylkill and its waters.

£.1500 for clearing and making navigable the Delaware, Lehigh and their waters.

Appropriations—April 13th. 1791.

Rivers, viz.

For the river Delaware,	£.3500
Lachawaxen,	250
Lehigh,	1000
Schuylkill,	2500
Susquehanna, from Wright's ferry to the mouth of Swatara creek, inclusive,	5250
From the mouth of Swatara to the mouth of Juniata,	300
From the mouth of Juniata to the mouth of the west branch,	300
Amount carried forward,	£.13100

T

	Amount brought forward,	£.13100
From the mouth of the weft branch to Starucca, at the great bend,		440
For the weft branch of Sufquehanna, from the mouth thereof to the Sinnamahoning,		160
For the Sinnamahoning to its north branch,		200
For the north branch of the Sinnamahoning as far as the place called Driftwood,		300
For the river Allegheny, from the place where the road from Driftwood will ftrike the fame, down to the mouth of Conewango creek,		150
For French creek, from its mouth to the portage leading to Prefqu' Ifle, on Lake Erie,		200
For the river Juniata, from the mouth to Water-ftreet,		820
From Water-ftreet to Franks town,		1500
For the Conemaugh, from Stoney-point to Richard's run,		400
From Richard's run through Chefnut ridge,		200
From Chefnut ridge to Loyal Hanning,		400
For the river Kifkiminetas, to the fecond falls inclufive,		250
From the faid falls to the river Allegheny,		100

Roads; April 13th. 1791.

From Stock Port, on the river Delaware, to Harmony on the river Sufquehanna,	400
From Drift-wood, on the Sinnamahoning, to the river Allegheny,	460
From French creek, to Prefqu' Ifle on Lake Erie,	400
Through the Canoe Narrows and from Daniel Titus's to Poplar run	300
From Poplar run, to Conemaugh,	360
From the forks of Little Conemaugh, to the mouth of Stoney creek,	180
For a road from the town of Wilkefbarree, to the Wind Gap,	500
From Harrifburgh, through the narrows, at the end of Kittatiny mountain and Peter's mountain, and from thence the neareft (and beft courfe to the place where it will interfect) to the road leading from Harrifburgh to Sunbury, at or near Halifax,	600
From Franks-town to Pittfburgh,	300
From Bedford to Pittfburgh,	500
From reading to Sunbury,	300
From Bedford to the weft fide of Laurel-hill,	400
From the mouth of Juniata, to David Miller's on the Juniata through Dick's Gap,	300
Through the Long Narrows,	180
Through Jacks and Igows narrows on the Juniata,	120
From near Cataweify, on the north branch of the Sufquehanna, to Hamburg on the river Schuylkill,	300
From York-town to Cooper's ferry, (to be applied between Muddy creek and the faid ferry)	100
From Fulton's ferry on the Sufquehanna towards Newport,	100
From Callender's mill over Croghan's Gap in the Blue mountain, to Weft's mill,	200

Amount carried forward, £.26420

Amount brought forward,	£. 26420
Through the upper part of Berks county down to Schuylkill,	300
From Keplinger's mill, on Little Schuylkill, to the Susquehanna,	300
Through Nicholls Gap, over the South mountain,	250
From Middle creek, to Grubb's furnace,	200
Through Black's Gap, over the South mountain,	100
From Buchanan's, on the east side of the South mountain and through the Great Cove, to the foot of Sideling-hill,	200
From Fort Penn, on the east-side of the north-west branch of Broadhead's creek to Wallenpaupeck, near the great falls, and from thence by or near the Indian orchard, between the river Delaware and Shohocking creek, to the river Susquehanna,	400

April 10th. 1792.

The monies appropriated by the act of April 13th. 1791, for opening the road from Poplar run to Conemaugh, and from little Conemaugh to the mouth of Stoney creek, and also from Franks-town to Pittsburgh, are resumed and applied as follows, to wit,

From Frankstown on Juniata, to Conemaugh, at or near Stoney creek, the sum of	530
And the remainder, from Conemaugh, at or near the mouth of Stoney creek, to the west side of the Chesnut ridge at or near Thomas Trimble's,	310
From Bedford to Pittsburgh, to be laid and applied to that part of the road between the east-side of Allegheny mountain, and the west-side of Laurel-hill,	800
From the east-side of Sideling-hill to the town of Bedford,	150
From Lehigh Water Gap, across the Matchunk mountain, to intersect the Nescopeck road made by Evan Owen,	200
Through Shippensburgh Gap over the South mountain leading towards York town,	200
Through M'Allister's Gap, to the Burnt Cabbins,	300
From Hughes's incampment, at the foot of the Dry ridge across the Allegheny mountain,	200
From Cherry's mill, on Jacob's creek, across the Chesnut ridge, thence to the top of Laurel hill, &c.	200
From the west end of High street, of the city of Philadelphia, through Blockley to the line of the county of Delaware,	300
For Vandering's hill, Roxbury township,	300
From Lancaster to Harrisburgh, beginning at the Bear,	500
From Shippensburgh to Bedford, over the three mountains,	200
From Mount-rock, near Carlisle, to Rankin's ferry on Susquehanna,	150
Across the Blue mountain at Smith's Gap, between the Wind Gap and the Lehigh Water Gap,	200
From Peter's mountain, on the east-side of Susquehanna to Sunbury, (in addition)	150
Amount carried forward,	£. 32860

Amount brought forward £.32900

From Wilkesbarre or Wyalusing or Mushoppen creek, and to intersect Ellicot's
road at or near Tioga point, - - - - 100
From Loyalsock creek, to the Tawanisco branch of Tioga, &c. - 100
From Stock Port on Delaware to Susquehanna near Mushoppen creek, - 100

Rivers; April 10th. 1792.

Monongahela, from the mouth thereof to the Virginia line, - £.1200
Youghiogeny from its mouth, to the mouth of Saltlick creek, - 1200
Juniata Rays-town branch, from the mouth thereof to Magaughey's mill, about
three miles above Bedford, and Dunning's creek from the mouth thereof
to the Big-fork, - - - - 600

Total £.36100

Note. These three sums, amounting to £.3000, are taken from the sum of £.4000 by the former act appropriated towards improving the navigation of the Little Conemaugh; but the faith of the state is pledged to make good the said sum of £.3000 whenever the Governor shall be of opinion, that the navigation of the Kiskiminetas and Conemaugh shall be so far improved, as to render the navigation of Little Conemaugh a necessary link in the chain of water and land communication between the eastern and western waters of the state.

Roads; April 11th. 1793.

From Philadelphia to York-town, through West-Chester, - Dollars, 400
From M'Call's ferry on Susquehanna, to the line of the Delaware state, by the
way of the cross roads, - - - - 300
From Prather's, on the top of Allegheny mountain in Bedford county, through
Berlin, to the west-side of the Chesnut-ridge, - - 300
From Spiker's, at the foot of the Allegheny, to Cherry's mill on Jacob's creek, 200
From Reading to Presqu' Isle, - - - - 1333
From Strasburgh in Lancaster county, to the line of the state of Delaware
towards Newport, - - - - 300
From the west-end of High street, Philadelphia, through Philadelphia county
to the line of Delaware county, - - - 200
From Perkioming to the Swamp meeting-house, - - 200
From Tohiccon to the Spring Field meeting house, - - 200
From Brackenridge's, to the Northampton county line, - 80
For a bridge over Perkioming creek, - - - 2300
For a bridge over Clark's Creek and Powel's creek, and for a road over Peter's
mountain from Ayre's farm to M'Call's tavern, - - 720
Road over Black's Gap and a bridge over Conegocheague creek, - 300
Bridges over Conegocheague creek and Conedogwinet creeks on the state road
from Shippensburgh to Bedford, - - - 300
From Burnt Cabbins to the east-side of Sideling hills, - 200
From Philadelphia to Sunbury (improving and compleating) from the Broad
mountain to Titeworth's tavern, - - - 800

Amount carried forward Dollars, 8133

	Amount brought forward, *Dollars*,	8133
Over Trent's Gap in Cumberland and York counties,		300
From Carlisle to Sherman's Valley to cross the north mountain near Hurley's Gap,		300
From Buffaloe hill, in Greenwood township, to the mouth of Wild Colt run,		200
From Spiker's to Cherry's mill,		300
From the top of Winding-ridge on the Maryland line, to the west-side of Laurel-hill near Union-town,		500
From near the line dividing the counties of Lancaster and Chester, on the north-side of the Welch mountain in the Paxton road, and from thence to the road leading from Philadelphia to the borough of York,		400
From M'Call's or Newberry's ferry, on Susquehanna, to intersect the road leading from Yorktown to Peach bottom ferry,		200
From Bedford to Pittsburgh,		500
From Franks-town to Pittsburgh,		500
From Wilkesbarre to Wyalusing,		700
From Fort Penn to the portage between Delaware river and Shohoking creek (in addition)		400
From Lehigh Water Gap, across the Matchunk mountain, to intersect the Nescopeck road (in addition)		400
From George Brown's, through the Little Gap of the Blue mountain,		200
Between Lewis town in Mifflin county and Huntingdon town,		400
From Lewis-town to Penn's valley,		400
From Peach bottom ferry, on Susquehanna, to the Maryland line towards Christiana,		500
	Total, *Dollars*,	14333

£200. appropriated by a former law towards opening and improving a road from Cherry's mill to the top of Laurel hill – applied towards opening and improving the road from Spiker's to Cherry's mill.

An act to enable the President and Managers of the Schuylkill and Susquehanna navigation, and the President and Managers of the Delaware and Schuylkill canal navigation, to raise, by way of lottery, the sum of four hundred thousand dollars, for the purpose of compleating the works in their acts of incorporation mentioned.

WHEREAS the companies incorporated for opening a canal and lock navigation, between the rivers Schuylkill and Susquehanna, and between the rivers Delaware and Schuylkill, have, from the novelty of such extensive and arduous undertakings, in a young country, experienced numerous difficulties beyond what were ever contemplated by the Legislature, at the time of passing the acts of incorporation, or by the subscribers to the said works, at the time of subscribing thereto: *And whereas* large sums of money have already been expended on the said works, and there is every reasonable expectation that a canal navigation, connecting the eastern and western waters of Pennsylvania, may be effectually compleated if efficient funds can be provided for the same, to the great advantage and increase of the agriculture, trade and manufactures of the state at large:

Section I. *Be it enacted by the Senate and House of Representatives of the commonwealth of Pennsylvania, in General Assembly met, and it is hereby enacted by the authority of the same,* That it shall and may be lawful to and for the Presidents and Managers, for the time being, of the said companies to raise, by way of lottery, a sum not exceeding two hundred and sixty-six thousand, six hundred and sixty-six dollars and sixty-seven cents, to be applied to carrying on the works of the Schuylkill and Susquehanna navigation, and one hundred and thirty-three thousand, three hundred and thirty-three dollars and thirty-three cents, to be applied to carrying on the works of the Delaware and Schuylkill canal navigation. *Provided always nevertheless,* That nothing herein contained shall be construed or held to authorize the said Presidents, Managers and Companies, or either of them, to form the said sum or sums into capital stock, or to consider them, or either of them, as any part of their capital stocks upon which a dividend of profits can be made.

Section II. *And be it further enacted by the authority aforesaid,* That the Presidents and Managers, previous to selling any tickets in the said lottery, shall lay the scheme thereof before the Governor of this commonwealth, to be approved of by him, and shall also enter into bonds to the Governor, for the due and faithful payment of all prizes that may be drawn in the said lottery, when the same shall be demanded, after the drawing of the said lottery shall be compleated.

Section

(80)

Section III. *And be it further enacted by the authority aforesaid*, That as soon as the said tickets shall be sold, the said Presidents and Managers shall certify the same to the Governor of the commonwealth, and, upon such certificate being presented, it shall and may be lawful for the Governor to appoint five Commissioners to superintend the drawing of the said lottery, which said Commissioners shall take an oath or affirmation, diligently and faithfully to perform the duties entrusted to them.

Section IV. *And be it further enacted by the authority aforesaid*, That the said Commissioners, or any three of them, shall attend at the drawing of each day, and, when the whole is compleated, shall cause an accurate list of the fortunate numbers to be published, in at least three news-papers in the city of Philadelphia, and the said Commissioners shall receive, of the Presidents and Managers of the said Companies, two dollars each for each day's attendance on the duties enjoined on them.

Section V. *And be it further enacted by the authority aforesaid*, That all prizes not demanded within twelve months after publication as aforesaid, shall be applied as aforesaid to carrying on and compleating the works of the said companies.

GEORGE LATIMER, *Speaker*
of the House of Representatives.

ROBERT HARE, *Speaker*
of the Senate.

Approved, April 17th. 1795.

THOMAS MIFFLIN, *Governor*
of the commonwealth of Pennsylvania.

PRINTED BY ZACHARIAH POULSON, JUNIOR.

www.ingramcontent.com/pod-product-compliance
Lightning Source LLC
Chambersburg PA
CBHW020155170426
43199CB00010B/1051